Campaign • 132

The First Crusade 1096–99

Conquest of the Holy Land

David Nicolle • Illustrated by Christa Hook

Series editor Lee Johnson • Consultant editor David G Chandler

First published in Great Britain in 2003 by Osprey Publishing,
PO Box 883, Oxford, OX1 9PL, UK
PO Box 3985, New York, NY 10185-3985, USA
Email: info@ospreypublishing.com

Osprey Publishing, part of Bloomsbury Publishing Plc

Transferred to digital print on demand 2015.

First published 2003
9th impression 2012

Printed and bound by PrintOnDemand-Worldwide.com,
Peterborough, UK.

A CIP catalogue record for this book is available from the
British Library.

ISBN: 978 1 84176 515 0

Editorial by Lee Johnson
Design by The Black Spot
Index by Alison Worthington
Maps by The Map Studio
3D bird's-eye views by The Black Spot
Battlescene artwork by Christa Hook
Originated by The Electronic Page Company, Cwmbran, UK

Dedication
For Fuad Kamal, fighter pilot, diplomat & artist.

Artist's note
Readers may care to note that the original paintings from which
the colour plates in this book were prepared are available for
private sale. All reproduction copyright whatsoever is retained
by the Publishers. All enquiries should be addressed to:

Scorpio
158 Mill Road,
Hailsham,
East Sussex
BN27 2SH
UK

scorpiopaintings@btinternet.com

The Publishers regret that they can enter into no
correspondence upon this matter.

The Woodland Trust
Osprey Publishing are supporting the Woodland Trust, the
UK's leading woodland conservation charity, by funding the
dedication of trees.

www.ospreypublishing.com

KEY TO MILITARY SYMBOLS

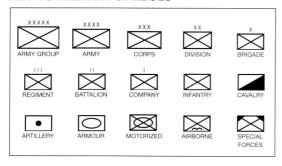

The First Crusade 1096–99

Conquest of the Holy Land

CONTENTS

ORIGINS OF THE CAMPAIGN   7

CHRONOLOGY   12

OPPOSING COMMANDERS   14

Crusader leaders • Byzantine leaders • Muslim leaders

OPPOSING FORCES   20

The Crusaders • The Byzantines • The Armenians • The Turks • The Fatimids

OPPOSING PLANS   27

The Crusader plan • Byzantine plans • Saljuq plans • Fatimid plans

THE CAMPAIGN   31

The ambush at Dorylaeum • The Crusade divides • The siege of Antioch
The march on Jerusalem • The siege of Jerusalem • The battle of Ascalon

THE AFTERMATH   88

THE BATTLEFIELDS TODAY   92

BIBLIOGRAPHY   94

INDEX   95

THE CHRISTIAN AND ISLAMIC WORLDS, C. AD1095

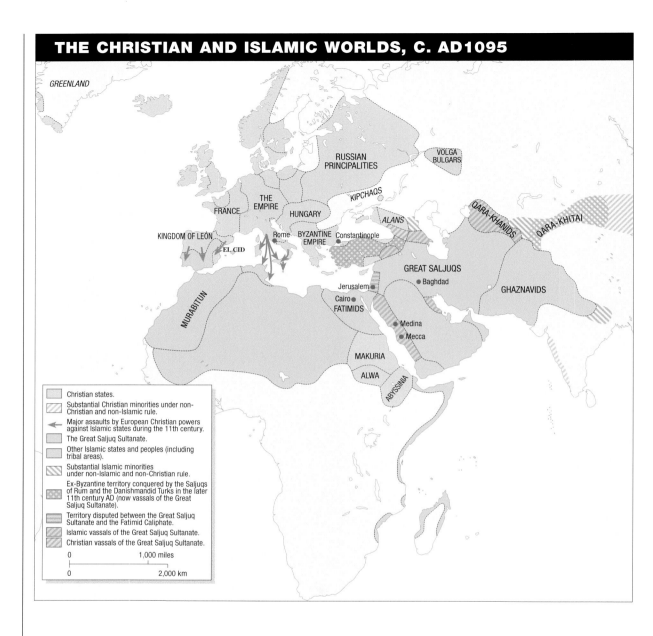

GREENLAND

RUSSIAN PRINCIPALITIES

VOLGA BULGARS

THE EMPIRE

FRANCE

HUNGARY

KIPCHAQS

QARA-KHANIDS

QARA-KHITAI

ALANS

KINGDOM OF LEÓN

Rome

BYZANTINE EMPIRE

Constantinople

EL CID

GREAT SALJUQS

Baghdad

GHAZNAVIDS

Jerusalem

Cairo

FATIMIDS

MURABITUN

Medina

Mecca

MAKURIA

ALWA

ABYSSINIA

Christian states.

Substantial Christian minorities under non-Christian and non-Islamic rule.

Major assaults by European Christian powers against Islamic states during the 11th century.

The Great Saljuq Sultanate.

Other Islamic states and peoples (including tribal areas).

Substantial Islamic minorities under non-Islamic and non-Christian rule.

Ex-Byzantine territory conquered by the Saljuqs of Rum and the Danishmandid Turks in the later 11th century AD (now vassals of the Great Saljuq Sultanate).

Territory disputed between the Great Saljuq Sultanate and the Fatimid Caliphate.

Islamic vassals of the Great Saljuq Sultanate.

Christian vassals of the Great Saljuq Sultanate.

0	1,000 miles
0	2,000 km

ORIGINS OF THE CAMPAIGN

In 1094 the Byzantine Emperor, Alexios I, came to the conclusion that Byzantium's own military and diplomatic efforts to regain lost territory in Anatolia were inadequate. Alexios decided to ask the Christian states of western Europe for support, which he did the following year. This can be seen as the genesis of what became the First Crusade.

Nevertheless, by 1095 the Byzantine Empire was not in such dire straits as has sometimes been suggested. Successes had been achieved since the Byzantine army's terrible defeat at Manzikert in 1071 and the Byzantine civil wars that followed. It was, in fact, the latter rather than the battle of Manzikert that allowed largely nomadic Turkish or Turcoman tribal peoples to take control of most of Anatolia. After Alexios seized the imperial throne he imposed a unified government on what remained of the Byzantine Empire and took advantage of divisions amongst its most threatening enemies to halt their advances, if not necessarily to defeat them. Byzantine rule was re-established in much of the Balkans while a potentially lethal alliance between the pagan Pecheneg Turks of south-eastern Europe and the Islamic Turkish *amir*, Çaka, was broken in 1091. Çaka had controlled Smyrna (Izmir) but was soon killed by another and more significant Turkish leader – Qïlïch Arslan I, ruler of the Saljuq Sultanate of Rum ('Rome' or ex-Byzantine Anatolia).

Byzantine efforts to reconquer Anatolia began the following year with a naval expedition under John Doukas to regain Aegean islands that had fallen to Çaka. Other campaigns removed rebel Byzantine

The Christian Monastery of Mar Matti (St Matthew) in northern Iraq, photographed in the early 1930s. (Photograph FILt Sharpe: St. Andrews University Library)

governors in Crete and Cyprus. Clearly the threat to Byzantium's age-old domination of the eastern seas was regarded as particularly dangerous. Relatively small-scale land and naval operations to regain part of the Anatolian mainland facing the Sea of Marmara and Black Sea were already under way and had achieved some local success when the First Crusade appeared on the scene.

Interestingly, several Islamic chroniclers saw 487AH (AD1094/95)[1] as a doom-laden year, including the later Mamluk historian Ibn Taghribirdi, who wrote: 'This year is called the year of the deaths of Caliphs and Commanders.' Those who died included the Fatimid Caliph al-Mustansir of Egypt, his Grand Vizier Badr al-Jamali, and the rival 'Abbasid Caliph al-Muqtadi in Iraq. The Great Saljuq Sultan Malik Shah and his Grand Vizier Nizam al-Mulk had already died in 1092. These deaths were followed by a period of confusion and near anarchy within the Islamic world. Rampant sectarianism divided Sunni Muslims from Shi'a Muslims and even amongst the Shi'a sects there were bitter rivalries. Furthermore the death of the Shi'a Fatimid, or Isma'ili, Caliph al-Mustansir was followed by a schism between supporters of his sons. The eldest, Nizar, was passed over as Caliph in favour of the younger, al-Musta'li. Nizar rebelled but was killed, after which his supporters formed the breakaway Nizari movement which, though still Isma'ili, became the so-called 'Assassins' of Iran and Syria. Although Islamic sectarian arguments might have seemed irrelevant to the Crusaders and even to the sophisticated Byzantines, they contributed further to the fragmentation and the weakened state of the Islamic Middle East when the First Crusade burst upon the scene in 1096.

The First Crusade is one of those dramatic episodes where historians cannot agree on 'causes'. All historical events are, of course, part of a chain and a historian's choice of 'background events' generally reflects his own

---

1 Islamic or *Hijri* years are indicated by the abbreviation AH. Being based on the lunar rather than solar cycle they were only 354 days long (a *Kabisa* or Islamic Leap Year being 355 days). Thus each *Hijri* year began on a different day of the Christian calendar. The *Hijri* year 487, a *Kabisa* year, began on 21 January, AD1094, and ended on 10 January, AD1095.

culture or sympathies. Some might claim that the First Crusade was 'caused' by the rise of Islam and its conquest of Palestine, the Christian Holy Land, in the 7th century AD. Others focus on a sequence of events beginning with the Byzantine Empire's reconquest of eastern Anatolia and northern Syria in the 10th century, regions that had been substantially Islamic for 300 years. The Byzantine Emperor's imposition of military control upon Armenia in eastern Anatolia in the mid-11th century, demilitarising the independent Armenian military aristocracy, unwittingly weakened the Empire's eastern frontier and permitted the Turkish breakthrough only a few decades later. Another significant event was the Saljuq Turkish conquest of most of the eastern and central parts of the Islamic world in the 11th century. This broke Shi'a political power in these regions and led to a revival of Sunni Islam, which was, eventually, a major factor in defeating the Crusading phenomenon. It also brought predatory and only superficially Islamic Turcoman tribes up to the eastern frontier of the Byzantine Empire.

A typical single-masted Mediterranean merchant ship as illustrated in a very stylised manner on an enamelled bronze door of the 12th-century Pala d'Oro. (*In situ* Cathedral of San Marco, Venice)

Following the Byzantine conquest, eastern and southeastern Anatolia became a militarised zone dominated by Byzantine garrisons. These garrisons included many soldiers from western and northern Europe, plus local Armenians, both Christian and followers of non-Christian, non-Islamic religions. Semitic Christians belonging to churches that both Greek and Catholic Europeans regarded as heretical were also represented.

The Byzantine annexation of Armenia had major military repercussions on both sides of the religious frontier. The Armenian state ruled by King Gagik II was placed under the Byzantine *Dux* or military governor of Iberia, which itself consisted of territory taken from independent Georgia. The heavy taxation imposed to pay for the Byzantine army and the consequent downgrading of the local Armenian feudal elite combined with religious differences between Byzantine Greeks and Armenians to create tension. Part of the Armenian military elite migrated north or west to independent Georgia or Byzantine Cappadocia respectively, while others crossed into Islamic territory.

Meanwhile epic changes were taking place in the neighbouring Islamic world with the arrival of the Saljuqs. They were a family or clan within a Turkish people called the Oghuz or Ghuzz. Their tradition of rule or authority was based upon power being shared within the family rather than being vested in one senior member. This system would, to some extent, be continued within the Great Saljuq Sultanate that they established in Iran, Iraq, Syria and some neighbouring areas. Although regarded by those Turks already living in the Islamic world as near barbarians, the Saljuqs' recent ancestors formed part of the vast Turkish people of Central Asia and had plenty of experience of building and running huge states. As the Saljuqs took over Iran they became very 'Persian' in culture and outlook and adopted a mystical, almost 'folk' form of Islam subtly different from the book-learned Islam characteristic of the Arab Middle East.

A Turcoman nomad encampment near Nigde in south-central Turkey. (Author's photograph)

The Saljuqs found the frontier with Byzantium poorly defended and many Turcoman and other raiders were able to operate deep inside Anatolia several years before the battle of Manzikert. Some were fighting as *ghazis*, or religiously motivated volunteers, seeking to regain territory lost to the Byzantines a century earlier, while others were simply free-booters. A major assault upon the seemingly powerful Byzantine Empire was not Saljuq policy and it was the Byzantine Emperor Romanos IV who initiated the major anti-Saljuq campaign that resulted in his own, and the Empire's, catastrophic defeat by the Great Saljuq Sultan Alp Arslan at Manzikert in 1071.

What followed was a gradual collapse of Byzantine authority across Anatolia, where many isolated Byzantine garrisons clung to fortified strongpoints while losing control of the countryside. It was neither a wholesale Turkish conquest nor a complete Byzantine withdrawal. Paradoxically the Turks were often invited to take over a city or area by claimants to the Byzantine throne in return for their military support. Alexios I himself had summoned Qïlïch Arslan's father, Sulayman, to Nicaea (Iznik).

The Great Saljuq Sultan Malik Shah took Qïlïch Arslan as a princely hostage after Sulayman's death. When Qïlïch Arslan was released and returned to Anatolia to re-assert Saljuq authority, he had great difficulty in doing so because other Turkish powers had arisen in the area, the most formidable being the Danishmandids.

From the 1070s to the appearance of the First Crusade, several Armenian leaders established ephemeral principalities in south-central Anatolia and along the northern fringes of Syria. Elsewhere parts of the old Armenian military elite, along with the descendants of Greek and western-European soldiers in Byzantine service, had accepted Turkish rule, adopting aspects of Turkish culture and language with many actually converting to Islam. Like the Christian Armenians they remained a distinct group and a significant military factor.

By the late 1090s the Great Saljuq state seemed to be in decline while local princes or governors fought amongst themselves. The death of the Great Saljuq Sultan Malik Shah in 1092 led the Fatimid Caliphate to attempt to regain Syria, and the decline in central Saljuq authority encouraged revolts amongst some previously dominant Arab tribes. This Fatimid effort failed and the Arabs were largely subdued but the entire region remained volatile. It is also important to note that Arab Christians of various sects remained a majority in several parts of the Middle East and formed substantial minorities elsewhere. There were large Jewish urban communities throughout the area and they played a significant political as well as cultural role under numerous Islamic rulers. In addition there were other notable religious communities whose beliefs were not Muslim, Christian or Jewish.

The idea that the Fatimid Caliphate based in Egypt was now in terminal decline is also misleading. The 10th century had seen the Fatimid high-water mark and much of the 11th had seen serious setbacks in Syria as well as famine and chaos within Egypt. This changed when Badr al-Jamali, a Fatimid general of Armenian origin who had converted to Islam, was invited to become Grand Vizier. Being Fatimid governor in Palestine at the time, he led his largely Armenian army to Cairo in 1074, restored order and thereafter ruled the state as a military dictator while the Caliph was little more than a puppet.

Badr al-Jamali was seemingly welcomed by the Coptic Church in Egypt and in return took a close interest in its affairs. He strengthened the long-established relationship between Fatimid Egypt and its African Christian neighbours in Nubia, Sudan and Ethiopia. Badr al-Jamali also retained strong links with his own Christian background and recruited large numbers of Christian Armenian soldiers. The other large element in the Fatimid army consisted of black Africans recruited as slaves through Christian Nubia or as mercenaries from Nubia and Sudan. Paradoxically it may thus have been true that a substantial part of the Fatimid army that faced the First Crusade was either Christian or had Christian origins. Badr al-Jamali's son, al-Afdal, succeeded him as Fatimid Grand Vizier, but unfortunately misread the motives of the First Crusade and suffered defeat in 1099.

CHRONOLOGY

1071

The Great Saljuq Sultan Alp Arslan defeats the Byzantine Emperor Romanos IV at the battle of Manzikert.

1074

Badr al-Jamali becomes Chief *Wazir* (Grand Vizier) and effectively military dictator of the Fatimid Caliphate.

1081

Alexios Komnenos becomes Emperor of Byzantium.

1092

Death of the Great Saljuq Sultan Malik Shah; civil war between his sons Mahmud and Berk Yaruq.

1093

Rebellion against the Great Saljuq overlordship by Tutush Ibn Alp Arslan, Saljuq ruler of Syria.

1094

Berk Yaruq Ibn Malik Shah becomes Great Saljuq Sultan (recognised as sole Sultan from December 1096); death of 'Abbasid Caliph al-Muqtadi in Baghdad, succeeded by al-Mustazhir; death of Fatimid Caliph al-Mustansir in Cairo, succeeded by child Caliph al-Musta'li; death of Fatimid Grand Vizier Badr al-Jamali, succeeded by his son al-Afdal.

1095

Kür-Bugha made governor of Mosul. Ridwan and Duqaq, the sons of Tutush, the late Saljuq ruler of Syria, seize Aleppo and Damascus respectively.

March: Council of Piacenza, Byzantine Emperor appeals to the West for help; Tutush of Syria defeated and killed by Sultan Berk Yaruq.

July (to Sept 1096): Pope Urban II journeys through France.

November: Council of Clermont, Pope Urban II preaches the Crusade for first time on 27 November.

December (to July 1096): Persecution of European Jews by Crusaders.

1096

Civil war between Ridwan of Aleppo and Duqaq of Damascus; Ridwan takes Ma'arat al-Nu'man from Yaghi Siyan of Antioch.

March: Departure of first wave of First Crusaders.

June (to August): First three waves of Crusader 'armies' broken up and dispersed in Hungary.

July: Crusade led by Walter-without-worldly-goods arrives in Constantinople (Istanbul).

1 August: Crusade led by Peter the Hermit arrives in Constantinople (Istanbul).

1 October: Peter the Hermit's Crusade defeated in Anatolia by Turkish Saljuqs of Rum.

23 December: Crusader force commanded by Godfrey of Bouillon arrives in Constantinople (Istanbul).

1097

Continuing civil wars between Saljuq rulers in Syria.

10 April: Godfrey of Bouillon swears fealty to Emperor Alexios and crosses to Anatolia.

14 May: Crusaders attack Saljuq of Rum capital of Nicaea (Iznik).

16 May: Crusaders drive off Saljuq attempt to relieve Nicaea.

19 June: Nicaea surrenders to Byzantine forces.

26–28 June: Crusader forces leave Nicaea.

1 July: Combined Turkish army of Saljuqs of Rum and Danishmandids defeated at so-called battle of Dorylaeum.

15 July: Genoese fleet departs for the eastern Mediterranean.

15 August: Crusaders take Iconium (Konya).

19 August: Anglo-Saxon fleet in Byzantine service seizes Latakia, probably from Banu 'Ammar of Tripoli.

27 September: Crusaders take Caesarea Mazacha (Kayseri).

13 October: Crusaders take Marash (Kahramanmaras).

21 October: Crusaders reach Antioch (Antakya) and begin siege.

Late October: Fleet of Guynemer of Boulogne takes the port of Latakia from Byzantine (Anglo-Saxon) garrison.

31 December: Crusaders defeat Saljuq force under Duqaq of Damascus at al-Bara.

Late 1097–early spring 1098: Byzantine army under John Ducas and Byzantine fleet under Admiral Caspax retake western Anatolia plus Lesvos, Chios and Samos; Byzantine army under Emperor Alexios advances to Philomelium (Aksehir).

Relief carving probably showing an Old Testament Patriarch dressed as a traveller or pilgrim, early 12th century. (*In situ* Cathedral, Autun; author's photograph)

1098

Early February: Byzantine general Tatikios withdraws his men from the siege of Antioch and rejoins Emperor Alexios at Philomelium.

9 February: Crusaders defeat Saljuq force under Ridwan of Aleppo at the Lake of Antioch.

March: Naval squadron consisting of Anglo-Saxon exiles in Byzantine service reaches port of Saint-Symeon (Samandagi).

10 March: Baldwin of Boulogne takes control of Edessa (Urfa).

3 June: Crusaders take city of Antioch (Antakya) but not its Citadel.

14 June: Crusaders discover supposed 'Holy Lance' in Antioch.

28 June: Crusaders defeat Saljuq Turkish relief army under Kür-Bugha of Mosul.

July: Ignorant of the Crusaders' defeat of Kür-Bugha, Emperor Alexios abandons his plan to march in their support and returns to Constantinople; Fatimid army retakes Jerusalem from Saljuq Turkish governor Sökmen Ibn Artuk.

11 December: Crusaders capture Ma'arat al-Nu'man and massacre the population.

1099

13 January: Raymond of Toulouse restarts the Crusader march south.

16 January: Raymond of Toulouse passes Shayzar without attacking.

28 January: Raymond of Toulouse seizes Hisn al-Akrad.

14 February–13 May: Raymond of Toulouse unsuccessfully besieges 'Akkar.

17 February: Crusaders seize Tortosa (Tartus).

16 May: Crusaders march past Tripoli (Trablus al-Sharqi in Lebanon).

26–29 May: Crusaders rest for four days outside Caesarea Palastina (Qaysariya).

1 June: Crusaders occupy Arsuf, turn inland towards Ramlah and Jerusalem; Fatimid garrison abandons and destroys the port of Jaffa.

2–6 June: Crusaders occupy Ramlah and reorganise for the march against Jerusalem.

6–7 June: Crusader force under Baldwin of Bourg and Tancred seizes Bethlehem.

7 June: Crusaders reach Jerusalem and begin siege.

16 June: Naval squadron of six Genoese ships enters the port of Jaffa; all except one are trapped by a larger Fatimid squadron.

15 July: Crusaders conquer Jerusalem from the Fatimid Caliphate.

22 July: Crusaders elect Godfrey of Bouillon as the ruler of Jerusalem.

9–11 August: Crusader army marches from Jerusalem against the Fatimid army outside Ascalon ('Askalan).

12 August: Crusaders defeat Fatimid army under al-Afdal outside Ascalon.

OPPOSING COMMANDERS

The First Crusade had no overall command. Nor did the Crusaders' Islamic foes. Only the Byzantine Empire had a united command under the Emperor.

CRUSADER LEADERS

The First Crusade was a collaborative effort by several contingents, each of which had its own leader. Nevertheless, certain figures emerged as more influential than others. Of these **Bohemond of Taranto** was perhaps the most effective military commander. A son of Robert Guiscard, the famous Norman conqueror of southern Italy, Bohemond was born in the 1050s and was originally christened Marc. The name Bohemond was that of a legendary giant and reflected the fact that the young Marc was physically large and strong. He was a great warrior and a devious politician willing to take on foes more powerful than him. Bohemond was still a teenager when he became a leader in his father's mercenary army. Realising that his stepmother would hinder his progress in favour of that of his half-brother Robert Borsa, Bohemond turned his attention to Byzantine territory but lost several clashes with the new Byzantine Emperor Alexios I.

In fact the preaching of the First Crusade came at good time for Bohemond of Taranto as it opened up opportunities in the east. The army that he took on Crusade was small, yet it had a big military impact. Immediately after the end of the First Crusade, during which he won control of Antioch, Bohemond was captured by the Turkish Danishmandid *amir*. After a prolonged captivity he was ransomed and, leaving his nephew Tancred as regent in Antioch, Bohemond returned to Italy where he renewed what had become a personal conflict with the Byzantine Emperor Alexios. A major campaign in 1105 ended with Alexios recognising Bohemond as Prince of Antioch while Bohemond accepted Alexios as his overlord. Bohemond died in southern Italy in March 1111 and was buried next to the Cathedral of Canosa.

Raymond of Saint-Gilles came from one of the oldest families in France. He was Count of Toulouse, Marquis of Provence, Duke of Narbonne and Count of Saint-Gilles, which was his main source of wealth. Nevertheless, he ended life simply as the Count of Tripoli in Lebanon. Why Raymond stayed in the east is something of a mystery. He was not in danger of losing his position in southern France, where he was one of the richest lords and a renowned warrior. Yet it is clear that he never intended coming back, swearing an oath to this effect, taking his wife with him and leaving his son as his successor in Toulouse. Unlike some other leaders of the First Crusade, Raymond of Saint-Gilles was inspired by religious motives. His

One of the earliest *mihrabs* or indicators for the direction of prayer in the university mosque of al-Azhar in Cairo, late 10th century. (Author's photograph)

14

army was large, well equipped and especially skilled in siege warfare, yet its military impact was less than expected.

Godfrey of Bouillon was born around 1061, the second son of Count Eustache II of Boulogne. His mother was the daughter of Duke Godfrey II of Lower Lorraine, but in 1076 the German Emperor refused to allow Godfrey of Bouillon to inherit his grandfather's Duchy, though he did become Duke in 1089. Continuing tensions with the German Emperor Henry meant that Godfrey of Bouillon might have been in danger of losing the Duchy at the time the First Crusade was preached. He thereupon sold or mortgaged most of his property before setting out for the east, probably not intending to return.

Godfrey did not play a particularly prominent role until the siege of Jerusalem, where his contingent was the first to break in. Godfrey of Bouillon was then selected as a compromise ruler of the newly conquered Holy City. He refused the title of king in the place 'where Christ had worn a Crown of thorns' accepting instead the title of Advocate of the Holy Sepulchre. Godfrey died in July 1100, being succeeded by his younger bother Baldwin. Within a few years Godfrey of Bouillon's life became the stuff of legend, particularly in the epic 'Crusade Cycle' written in the 12th century.

Count Robert of Flanders was extremely rich and seems to have had no secular ambitions in the east. He apparently went on Crusade for religious reasons and always intended to come home. **Count Robert of Normandy** similarly clearly planned to come home. He was the eldest son of Duke William of Normandy, King William the Conqueror of England, and had twice been designated heir of his father's domains but each time ruined his prospects by rebellion. Robert did, however, become Duke of Normandy when William the Conqueror died in 1087. He then tried to overthrow his brother William II as King of England. By the time Robert of Normandy returned in 1100, his younger brother had succeeded as King Henry I of England. Robert made another attempt to gain the crown, failed, lost Normandy to Henry I and died as a prisoner in Cardiff castle in 1134.

Baldwin of Boulogne was a more successful character. Joining the Crusade with his brothers Godfrey of Bouillon and Eustace III of Boulogne, he was at first a minor figure with a minimal power-base. Presumably for this reason, Baldwin of Boulogne had high ambitions from the start, carving out a state for himself as soon as the Crusade reached Syria. This became the County of Edessa. When Godfrey of Bouillon died, Baldwin succeeded his brother and was crowned King of Jerusalem.

Count Stephen of Blois was one of the richest men to go on the First Crusade. His motives seem to have been largely religious, though Stephen was also bullied into going by his domineering wife Adela, a daughter of William the Conqueror. He had no intention of staying in the east and actually came home before the conquest of Jerusalem, whereupon his wife made him go again to complete his pilgrimage vow.

A ceramic bowl from Nishapur in Iran, showing a horseman with an axe and wearing full armour including a mail coif, 10th–11th century. (Reza Abbasi Museum, Tehran; author's photograph)

Ruins of the Old Mosque at Salamiya in Syria, which was built in AD1088. It contains the tomb of one of the 'hidden *imams*' of the Isma'ili Islamic sect. A 'hidden *imam*' is believed to have been one of the hereditary spiritual leaders of the Isma'ili movement who, because he lived in a time of persecution, never made himself public. The first Fatimid Caliph, 'Ubaid Allah, was also born in Salamiya in the late 9th century AD. (Author's photograph)

Of those men who rose from obscurity during the First Crusade, the most ruthless was probably **Tancred**. His father was a Norman, Odo 'The Good Marquis', in southern Italy and his mother was a daughter of Robert Guiscard. Little is known about Tancred's early life though he probably learned Greek and Arabic. His uncle, Bohemond of Taranto, persuaded him to join the Crusade in 1096. Tancred probably accompanied the main army to Palestine while Bohemond remained at Antioch because he feared being overshadowed by his uncle. Tancred then spent the rest of his life as Prince of Galilee, regent of Antioch during Bohemond's long captivity, and in attempts the win territory from his Muslim and Christian neighbours. He died in 1112.

BYZANTINE LEADERS

Emperor Alexios Komnenos I reigned from April 1081 to his death in August 1118. The son of John Komnenos, he began his career as a general under the Emperors Michael VII and Nikephoros III. Alexios and his brother turned against Nikephoros and in February 1081 took the imperial capital, Constantinople. Alexios came to the throne with the support of the Byzantine military aristocracy, his formidable wife Irene also coming from a powerful military family, the Doukai. His successes were partly military and partly diplomatic. Alexios I also attempted to reshape the entire ruling class of Byzantium with as much centralised power in his hands as possible. Though genuinely pious, Alexios also resisted Church interference in government affairs.

Tatikios, who accompanied the First Crusade to Antioch, had an interesting background and a remarkable career. Born around 1057, his father was described as a 'Saracen' captured by John Komnenos, the father of Emperor Alexios. Tatikios is generally regarded as the first Turk to achieve high command in the Byzantine army. Crusader sources state that his nose had been 'cut off' or slit – the mark of a slave in the Byzantine Empire. Though first mentioned merely as a scout, Tatikios was raised to the rank of *Grand Primikerios* by Emperor Alexios. During the campaign against Norman invaders in the Balkans, he commanded 'Turks living around Ochrida'. Between 1086 and 1095 he fought against Pecheneg Turks in the Balkans and Saljuq Turks in Anatolia, being praised for skill, foresight and competence in commanding Turkish and western European mercenary troops. In his role as commander of the Byzantine contingent that accompanied the Crusaders across Anatolia, he served as Alexios' representative and received the surrender of various towns in the Emperor's name.

MUSLIM LEADERS

Qïlïch Arslan I, son of Sulayman Ibn Qutalmïsh, was the second Saljuq ruler of Anatolia. He was in Antioch when his father was killed fighting against Tutush of Syria and was then handed over to the Great Saljuq Sultan Malik Shah. Following the latter's death in 1092 Qïlïch Arslan escaped and returned to Nicaea in Anatolia where he was accepted as sovereign by the Turcomans fighting the Byzantines. He was, however, more interested in achieving good relations with Saljuq rulers to the east than in attacking Byzantium.

Although Qïlïch Arslan defeated the Peasants' Crusade, he was himself defeated by the 'official' First Crusade. Forced to abandon Nicaea, Qïlïch Arslan established a longer-lasting capital in Konya. He is, in fact, credited with establishing the flourishing Saljuq Sultanate of Rum, which endured until the early 14th century. Qïlïch Arslan was respected by Christian and Muslim subjects because of his tolerance and his reviving of the shattered Anatolian economy. He was killed in battle in 1107.

Yaghi Siyan, the ruler of a small state around Antioch, was the only early Saljuq governor still in place when the First Crusade arrived, having been appointed around 1090. Yaghi Siyan's territory was extended, probably by Tutush of Syria, to include Manbij and Tal Bashir but he was frequently hostile to Ridwan, the son of Tutush who took control of Aleppo in 1095. This hostility had a profound impact on the First Crusade.

The Tomb of Bohemond of Taranto next to the Cathedral in Canosa di Puglia, southern Italy. (Author's photograph)

The eastern or Asiatic shore of the Bosporus, seen from Istanbul on the European side. By the time the First Crusade arrived, the Byzantine army had regained this shore and some territory beyond. (Author's photograph)

Ridwan Ibn Tutush of Aleppo is generally portrayed in a negative light by Arab chronicles, being blamed for the divisions that made the Crusader invasion easier. Most of these chroniclers were Sunni Muslims, so Ridwan's brief flirtation with the Shi'a of Syria and with the Fatimid Caliphate was similarly criticised. In fact, Ridwan did manage to make enemies of practically all his neighbours, including his father-in-law and *atabeg*, Janah al-Dawla Husayn, as well as his brother Duqaq of Damascus. Under such circumstances it is hardly surprising that Ridwan looked for allies wherever he could find them, including the Shi'a. Nevertheless he retained power until his death in 1113.

Kür-Bugha was a powerful Saljuq *amir* who supported Berk Yaruq in the struggle between Malik Shah's sons. He was captured and imprisoned in Syria, but when Berk Yaruq was victorious Kür-Bugha was released and appointed governor of Mosul in 1095. He remained governor of this important city, representing the Great Saljuq Sultan's interests in the fragmented western part of the empire. However, Kür-Bugha's power was resented by several other Saljuq governors and princes and after his defeat by the Crusaders outside Antioch his prestige declined. Kür-Bugha's death in 1102 led to further disruption and a civil war in northern Iraq.

The revival seen in the Fatimid Caliphate of Egypt started under the authoritarian rule of the Muslim-Armenian Grand Vizier Badr al-Jamali. It continued under his less militaristic son, the **Grand Vizier al-Afdal Ibn Badr al-Jamali**. Born around 1066, his original name was Abu'l-Qasim Shahanshah. Better known as al-Afdal, he took over as vizier during his father's final illness in 1089 and, as the biographer Ibn Khallikan put it,

The front and back of a coin struck in the name of King Baldwin I of Jerusalem. As Baldwin of Boulogne and then as Count of Edessa, Baldwin had been one of the more minor leaders of the First Crusade.

A fragment of 11th- or early 12th-century painted paper from the ruins of Fustat on the outskirts of Cairo, showing a turbaned soldier with a shield and two javelins. (Museum of Islamic Art, Cairo; author's photograph)

The Byzantine Emperor Alexios I, as portrayed on an early 12th-century mosaic. (*In situ*, Aya Sofia, Istanbul)

'was an able ruler possessing a superior judgement'. When the Fatimid Caliph al-Musansir died in 1094, al-Afdal virtually confined the new Caliph al-Musta'li in his palace while he himself governed the Fatimid state. Al-Musta'li died 1101 and was succeeded by a child, al-Amir, but when latter grew up he had the overmighty al-Afdal assassinated in 1121. This ended 27 years of internal peace and only limited conflict with the newly established Crusader Kingdom of Jerusalem. Al-Afdal's financial reforms greatly increased the wealth of the Fatimid state but at the same time the Grand Vizier accumulated vast wealth for himself.

Little is known about **Iftikhar al-Dawla**, the commander of the Fatimid garrison in Jerusalem at the time of the Crusader assault. He was mentioned as governor of Ascalon immediately after the fall of Jerusalem, suggesting that he had been governor of all Fatimid Palestine in 1099. It is also possible that Iftikhar had been one of the elite slave-recruited soldiers of the previous Grand Vizier, Badr al-Jamali. According to the Syrian Christian chronicler Bar Hebraeus, the Fatimid governor of Jerusalem was; 'a man from the quarter of the Egyptians whose name was 'Eftekhar ad-Dawla'. This could indicate that he was of Nubian or Sudanese origin since men of Arab or Turkish descent are normally specified as such. Iftikhar al-Dawla is also unlikely to have been a Berber since such men were usually called Arabs in sources like Bar Hebraeus.

The name Iftikhar al-Dawla is quite rare and might indicate adherence to Shi'a rather than Sunni Islam. A man with this name, and of roughly the right age, is mentioned in Usamah Ibn Munqidh's famous autobiography. Usamah was brought up in Shayzar overlooking the river Orontes in western Syria. He relates how an *amir* or senior officer, perhaps retired, named Iftikhar al-Dawla Abu'l-Futuh Ibn 'Amrun was lord of the nearby castles of Abu Qubays, Qadmus and al-Kaf, and whose sister was also married to Usamah's uncle, the ruler of Shayzar.

OPPOSING FORCES

THE CRUSADERS

According to the *Gesta Francorum*, the Fatimid Grand Vizier al-Afdal described the victorious Crusaders as, 'a force of beggars, unarmed and poverty-stricken, who have nothing but a bag and a scrip.' This reflects the Crusaders' self-image as a host of 'poor pilgrims'. The Pope had, however, emphasised the need for material preparation and the Crusaders' responsibility to ensure their dependants were properly cared for. The participants grouped themselves around the most senior lords present though most of those involved were relatively prosperous.

Many nationalities were represented on the First Crusade, though the bulk seemed content to be described as Franks – even those who were not French. Perhaps the term still reflected a sort of pan-western Christian solidarity. One major group was the Provençals from southern France and there is strong evidence that these southerners felt themselves to be different from the northern French and Normans. The so-called Normans of southern Italy included men of genuine Norman origin, plus Bretons, Flemings, Poitevins and a few Angevins. The number of real Italians was very small within the 'land' contingents, though Italians played a dominant role in naval forces. A Lotharingian-German element in Godfrey of Bouillon's contingent was again greatly outnumbered by Flemings and men from French-speaking Artois.

When the Pope preached the Crusade he called for knights and foot soldiers, and there were clearly more infantry than cavalry even at the

The ruined medieval walls of Malatya in east-central Turkey. (Author's photograph)

The fortified brick walls and one of the Byzantine gates of Nicaea (Iznik). (Frederick Nicolle photograph)

start of the First Crusade. Many were prosperous peasants who could pay their own way and had proper military equipment. Even so properly equipped fighting men were probably in a minority on the First Crusade, many not being armed at all. Non-combatants included clerics and monks who had been given permission to go on Crusade, while some women also accompanied their husbands. In fact the presence of large numbers of women and children sometimes caused problems and many died on the way. The lowest modern estimate for the size of the First Crusade when it assembled at Constantinople is 30,000 people.

The composition of the forces that marched east as the First Crusade may have been unlike normal western European armies but their organisation was similar, with members of the aristocracy assuming military and diplomatic leadership. This was accepted even by men from urban backgrounds since, with a few exceptions in Italy, the cities of western Europe still operated within a generally, though sometimes only theoretically, 'feudal' framework. Other lower-ranking Crusaders attached themselves to the retinue of a recognised leader. On a few occasions ordinary knights or 'the poor' grouped themselves around one of their own number, for example the ferocious *Tafurs*. Others, especially infantry, may have fought and marched in 'national' groups reflecting their place of origin.

Although the official First Crusade demonstrated much greater discipline than the so-called 'Peasants' Crusade', it was still more of a host than an army, being characterised by a divided command and a very loose structure. Many people, especially amongst the camp followers, were apparently without effective leaders. The strictly military elements of this Crusading host were organised around lords and their households, and most of the 'commoners' may actually have been dependent relatives. The strong bonds of companionship seen between men in the knightly elite have sometimes been interpreted as latently or actually homosexual but

this is incorrect since the ideals of male comradeship were fundamental to the knightly way of life, social structure and general ethos as well as methods of combat.

The Italians played a significant role by providing the naval support without which the First Crusade would probably not have succeeded. Amalfi had been the first Italian state to emerge as a significant naval power but it rarely took part in offensive operations against Islamic shipping or coasts; equally Venice was more concerned with the Byzantine Empire. By contrast Pisa and Genoa had already being carrying out an unofficial naval 'Crusade' against the Islamic states for decades.

THE BYZANTINES

The loss of most of Anatolia deprived the Byzantine Empire of a major pool of military manpower. As a result, at the end of the 11th century foreign troops may have outnumbered domestic recruits. The latter, however, included refugees from the lost eastern provinces, the sons of 'fallen men' and recruits from those regions still held by the Byzantines. Those who did not speak Greek included Bulgars and Serbs from the Balkans, but Turkish recruits were becoming increasingly important. They included survivors of the defeated Pechenegs in the Balkans, Turks from northwestern Anatolia who had been 'turned' by the Emperor Alexios, converting to Christianity as part of their change of allegiance. The *Rhos* who served in Byzantine armies were probably from the Scandinavian aristocracy that dominated a large part of Russia.

All western European recruits were mercenaries during this period. Large numbers of such western troops had garrisoned the eastern frontier before the later 11th-century collapse, many subsequently remaining there. Later recruits included French, Danes, Saxons from Germany, Pisans and Ligurians from Italy, Frisians, Flemings, Hungarians, and Anglo-Saxon refugees from the Norman conquest of England. Normans were themselves prominent in the late 11th-century Byzantine army. Most came from the newly established Norman Kingdom in southern Italy.

Here it is worth noting that at the start of Alexios' reign the Byzantine army was desperately short of cavalry horses, so the new Emperor bought remounts in Islamic Syria, probably from the Fatimid-ruled coastal region. This is further evidence of a close and generally friendly relationship between the Fatimid Caliphate and the Byzantine Empire, both of which felt threatened by the Saljuq Turks.

The Byzantine army of the late 11th and 12th centuries consisted of two main forces, one in the European and one in the Asian provinces under the overall command of the 'Grand Domestic'. Infantry and cavalry were still divided into light and heavy regiments, these largely organised according to ethnic origin. The army was further divided into central and provincial forces. Another senior officer called a *sebaste* commanded 'foreign' troops, probably meaning those not fully integrated into the Byzantine military structure. However, Byzantine provincial forces never recovered from the disasters of the late 11th century.

The lost stained-glass windows in the Church of St Denis, Paris, dating from the mid-12th century though now known only from these 18th-century engravings. A: The Turks defeated outside Nicaea. B: The Crusaders capture Nicaea.

THE ARMENIANS

After the Byzantine disaster at Manzikert in 1071 the Armenians had to look after themselves and several cities established local militias. For many years a senior ex-Byzantine officer named Philaretus also resisted the Saljuqs in the mountains north of Antioch. His army largely consisted of Armenians plus an elite of ex-Byzantine Norman mercenaries. At the same time there was a massive migration by the Armenian military elite from eastern Anatolia into the mountains bordering Cilicia. This became the heartland of a new Cilician Armenian kingdom, the most effective part of whose army consisted of light cavalry and infantry archers. However, the most significant 11th-century Armenian migrations involved urban elites. Such men dominated Edessa (Urfa) before the arrival of the First Crusade, by which time the city was highly militarised and possessed an effective local militia.

Other Armenian families migrated into Islamic areas where they fought for both Turkish and Arab rulers. Just as some Turks converted to Christianity and fought for Byzantium, many Armenians became Muslims. According to the Crusader chronicler Raymond of Aguillers, many Armenians and Greeks had *turcaverant* or 'become Turks' and helped defend Antioch. Other Armenians supported Yaghi Siyan without abandoning Christianity.

Apart from Christians and Muslims, the Armenians included other more obscure religious communities including the *Arewordik* or 'Children of the Sun'. They seem to have clung to a pre-Christian Armenian religion very similar to Iranian Zoroastrianism.

The interior of the Istanbul Gate of Iznik. (Frederick Nicolle photograph)

THE TURKS

Even before the arrival of the Saljuqs, slave-recruited Turkish *ghulams* had been highly trained and valuable troops. They were very expensive to hire and to equip since they used a lot of armour but could defeat

A naval battle illustrated in the 11th-century Byzantine *Cynegetica of Pseudo-Oppianos.* (Biblioteca Marciana, Cod. Gr. 479, f. 23r, Venice)

much larger forces of local infantry and light cavalry. In fact military recruitment in the Islamic world continued to reflect earlier traditions until the coming of the Mongols in the 13th century. Even the tribal Saljuqs turned to traditional methods of recruitment as they spread their authority over much of the Middle East.

A famous treatise on government written by the Saljuq Grand Vizier Nizam al-Mulk, reflected traditional attitudes by advocating a mixed army including Daylamis, Khurasanis, Georgians and Farsis to avoid the threat of rebellion. In fact many of the first so-called Turks to break into Byzantine Anatolia included Persians, Daylamis and Kurds as well as Turks. Non-Turks certainly played an important role in the armies of various minor leaders in 11th-century Syria while the urban militias of northern Syria and the Jazirah (northern Mesopotamia) defended their walls for and against the Turks.

Later Saljuq armies tended to be small, usually no more than 10,000–15,000 men, and even smaller armies characterised the autonomous states of the Fertile Crescent as the Great Saljuq Sultanate fragmented. Typically their rulers could only afford a small *'askar* bodyguard of slave-recruited *ghulams* or *mamluks*, around which a larger force of *ajnad* provincial troops could assemble. *Ahdath* urban militias still played a role and in many areas Turkish and Arab women not only fought in defence of their homes but donned full armour when necessary. In a crisis the rulers of larger Syrian cities could also summon 'allied' Turcoman nomad warriors from as far away as northern Mesopotamia.

Most Turks in 11th-century Anatolia were only superficially Muslim. Yet the Byzantine chronicler and princess, Anna Komnena, regarded them as more chivalrous and civilised than the 'Franks' and Crusaders. The Saljuqs of Rum who ruled west-central Anatolia attempted to model their army on that of their Great Saljuq predecessors in Iran. Nevertheless, at the time of the First Crusade their military forces largely consisted of Turcoman tribesmen around a tiny professional elite of slave-recruited *ghulams*. The latter came from many backgrounds including Greek prisoners of war. Much of the old Byzantine frontier elite had also entered the new military class while mixed Greek–Turk soldiers were already important in the Saljuq Rum army. A similar process occurred under the Danishmandid *amirs* who ruled east-central Anatolia.

Theoretically the Great Saljuq Sultanate was divided into 24 military zones, each commanded by an officer who had to raise, train and equip a specified number of local troops then lead them to a military review each spring. However, this proved unattainable and the Saljuq Sultans had to hire mercenaries and demand contingents from local vassals.

The armies of the small Saljuq principalities in Syria were probably similar to that of better-documented 12th-century Damascus. It was divided into five sections according to the soldiers' origins or role. The ruler's own elite palace units formed an *askar* of regular cavalry. Regular troops lived within the city while tribal forces summoned for a single campaign camped in the irrigated area outside. The militia and *mutatawwi'a* religious volunteers were paid, being more like a permanent, though part-time, force rather than short-term auxiliaries.

'Guard of King Herod' on a German carved wooden doorway made around AD1065. (*In situ* north transept of the Church of S. Maria im Kapitol, Cologne)

The battle of Dorylaeum as illustrated in the lost mid-12th-century windows in the Church of St Denis, Paris.

Even in the 1970s many major routes in central Turkey were still unsurfaced, including this dusty road through a valley where the First Crusade itself passed. (author's photograph)

THE FATIMIDS

The most significant military development in traditional Middle Eastern armies was the increase in the proportion of professional personnel. The level of skill demanded of a soldier was now so high that the old militias and tribal forces could no longer compete. This was clearly seen in the Fatimid Caliphate whose recruitment and structure had changed considerably since the Fatimid conquest of Egypt and Syria in the 10th century. Its army was more effective than is generally thought but was also smaller; the biggest later-Fatimid armies being some tens of thousands.

The majority of soldiers may have been Sunni Muslim, despite the fact that the Fatimid Caliphate was a Shi'a state, and most of the contingents that played a prominent role in the early days had been downgraded in favour of new sources of recruitment. Virtually all Berber units were, for example, disbanded by the Armenian Grand Vizier Badr al-Jamali in AD1073, although naval troops still included Berbers and Arabs. African troops now played a major role in Fatimid forces, especially as garrison infantry. The loyalty of slave-recruited African troops was such that they formed elite armoured infantry guards for more than one Fatimid Caliph. Other *sudani* or 'blacks', as they were called in the Arabic sources, included mercenaries from Nubia, Eritrea, Ethiopia and beyond.

Though fewer in number, Arab troops of Bedouin origin played an influential role. In fact it was largely Arab soldiers from southern Palestine who enabled the Fatimid outpost of Ascalon to hold out against the invading Crusaders for so long. Non-Bedouin local Arab populations had a limited military role under the Fatimids, normally in urban *ahdath* militias, although these were more typical of Syria and Palestine than Egypt. It is also worth noting that the substantial Jewish population of Jerusalem had close connections with the Fatimid garrison at the time of the First Crusade, and also fought in defence of the city's walls.

Experience of fighting Turkish *mamluks* or *ghulams* in Syria and Palestine rapidly convinced the Fatimid Caliph that he should build a new army on the same pattern as that of his eastern rivals. Not surprisingly these eastern foes did not want elite Turkish *mamluk* recruits to reach the Fatimids and so the latter were unable to purchase as many as they wished. As a result, the elite of the later Fatimid army was a mixture of prisoners of war and mercenaries. It is also possible that part of the Saljuq garrison in Jerusalem was re-employed by the Fatimids after they retook the city in 1098.

The Fatimids recruited Armenians in larger numbers as both infantry archers and cavalry. In fact Armenian troops became so important that several Grand Viziers were selected from their commanding officers in the late 11th and 12th centuries. They probably formed at least half of the Cairo garrison and would play a significant role in Ascalon during the early 12th century. It seems likely that the presence of Armenian *ghulams* in Fatimid service also made it easy for Armenian refugees to find employment during the second half of the 11th century. Their main role was to defend Egypt against the Saljuq Turks and then to launch a counter-attack to regain Syria.

Daylami infantry also reached Egypt, where they were particularly welcome because they, like the Fatimid Caliphs, were Shi'a Muslims. These professional soldiers may also have formed the Fatimid army's *naffatun*, an elite corps of 'fire-troops'. A famous description by Ibn al-Tuwayr of the Fatimid regiments who paraded during a New Year celebration in the late 11th or early 12th century even included an infantry unit said to consist of 'Franks' – namely western Europeans.

Once the Fatimids had conquered Egypt in the 10th century they attempted to copy classic 'Abbasid military organisation, maintaining a substantial garrison in their new capital of Cairo. But the bulk of the Fatimid army was stationed in Syria until this fell to the Saljuq Turks in the 11th century. Thereafter the Fatimids struggled grimly to maintain their control of the coasts of Palestine and what is now Lebanon, a situation that was ongoing when the First Crusade arrived in AD1099.

The Fatimid army itself consisted of regiments identified either by the ruler who raised them, by the name of their commanding officer or by their technical function. Such regiments were subdivided into smaller units down to groups of ten men and there were well-established officer ranks; most of the complex military administration was carried out by Coptic Christian scribes.

OPPOSING PLANS

THE CRUSADER PLAN

Historians still argue about what the First Crusade originally intended to achieve and whether there was a clear objective when, in 1095, Pope Urban II started preaching what became the First Crusade. However, a more traditional interpretation of the origins of the First Crusade maintains that the Crusade and the Crusading Vow always focused upon going to Jerusalem and taking the Christian Holy Land from the 'infidel' Muslims. At the same time it seems clear that the Latin, Catholic or western European Church had two aims, namely to help the Byzantine Empire and to conquer Jerusalem. The first of these aims would hopefully inspire gratitude in the Orthodox Greek or eastern Christian world and thus facilitate the reunification of Christendom under Papal leadership following the Latin–Orthodox Schism of 1054.

By the time the First Crusade marched east its primary aim was to conquer the Holy Land, while helping the Byzantine Empire recover lost territory now seemed secondary. Earlier, when the primary aim may have been to assist the Emperor Alexios, the question of Crusaders' relations with Islamic peoples and states was not important. They were simply an enemy to be defeated. Quite what was expected to happen once Jerusalem was captured was, however, unclear. What, for example, would happen to the Islamic populations of the area? There may have been a vague hope that the Islamic world could be converted to Christianity, though the evidence for this is thin. In an atmosphere of increasing religious

The medieval walls and towers of Kayseri in Cappadocia, south-central Turkey. (Author's photograph)

A seated Saljuq Turkish ruler surrounded by attendants and guards, on an 11th-century stucco wall decoration from Rayy, Iran. (Archaeological Museum, Tehran; author's photograph)

excitement, questions concerning 'after Jerusalem' may have seemed irrelevant to ordinary Crusaders, though not to those who planned to stay in the east. It is worth noting that Crusader leaders who later established themselves in the Middle East avoided taking too strong an oath of allegiance to the Byzantine Emperor in Constantinople whereas those who subsequently went home apparently had no trouble in doing so. Plans also changed or evolved during the course of the First Crusade and, after their remarkable early successes, many Crusaders came to see themselves as fighting to expand Christianity rather than merely to conquer the Holy Land.

The Crusade was not a development of earlier large-scale pilgrimages, though it may initially have been mistaken as such by many in the Middle East. Earlier pilgrims had been penitents and were normally unarmed. The Crusaders were performing a 'penance in arms', which was new and revolutionary. Their strategy was relatively straightforward though ambitious. Concepts of 'the East' and 'Jerusalem' seem to have been virtually one and the same amongst the majority of people in late 11th-century western Europe, but several who marched east already knew the road. Some had been to Jerusalem as pilgrims and others were veterans of mercenary service in the Byzantine army.

BYZANTINE PLANS

The Emperor Alexios I probably had a clear strategy in mind when he requested military assistance from the West. He needed troops to expand the campaign of reconquest that had already started in Anatolia and he wanted to regain as much of the territory lost since the battle of Manzikert as possible. Unfortunately the Crusader hosts that arrived outside Constantinople were not what Alexios had in mind. They were not mercenaries or even military volunteers willing to serve under Byzantine command. Instead they were a potential threat to the stability of the Empire. While fearing their trouble-making potential and soon suspecting that several leaders intended to seize territory for themselves rather than winning it back for Byzantium, Alexios used his political, diplomatic and military skill to channel the Crusaders' potential in useful directions. In this he was at least partially successful.

Byzantine strategy was clearly aimed at denying the Saljuq Turks of Anatolia access to the sea, most immediately to the small Sea of Marmara facing Constantinople. Here the Byzantine army and navy had already achieved some success. It is also worth noting that the Fatimid Caliphate was equally keen to deny the Saljuq Turks access to the Mediterranean in Syria, Lebanon and Palestine. This similarity of strategic interests has not been recognised by most historians but may have contributed to those diplomatic exchanges between Constantinople and Cairo during the course of the First Crusade.

In the event the Crusaders were almost immediately persuaded to abandon the traditional pilgrim road through Ancyra (Ankara). Instead they followed Byzantine advice and took an unusual southerly route through arid and empty terrain. Alexios saw possession of Antioch in Pisidia (Yalvaç) as the key to the province of Pisidia. Thus he regarded the Crusaders' march as part of a broader campaign by Byzantine forces to retake western Anatolia.

The Emperor may also have hoped to use the Crusader horde to reconstruct a strong pro-Byzantine Armenian principality around Antioch and the Taurus mountains. Consequently the Crusaders were persuaded to again leave the direct 'pilgrim road' to Jerusalem and march through Marash (Kahramanmaras). This apparent diversion also separated Yaghi Siyan in Antioch from the Saljuqs of Rum to his north.

SALJUQ PLANS

There was no overall Islamic plan to deal with the Crusaders. The invasion not only came as a complete surprise to the Muslims but there was, as yet, virtually no understanding of what the Crusade was all about. Consequently the Saljuq Turkish states reacted to it independently. Qïlïch Arslan, the ruler of the Saljuqs of Rum, had easily defeated the Peasants'

In summer the mountains and valleys of the Taurus mountains are fertile and benign, but in winter it would have been extremely difficult to take a medieval army though such terrain. (Author's photograph)

Crusade and seems to have expected to deal similarly with the First Crusade. Following the defeats of the temporary Saljuq/Danishmandid alliance at Nicaea and Dorylaeum (Eskisehir), Qïlïch Arslan allowed the Crusaders to pass through his territory. This may indicate that he had grasped their real intention. In the event he was able to retake considerable territory after the Crusaders moved on. He may also have realised the Byzantines represented the greater threat to the Saljuqs of Rum, and sought to devote his remaining strength and authority to limiting the Byzantine reconquest.

While the Danishmandid *amir* recognised that the Crusade was no real threat to his territory in north-central Anatolia, the Saljuq Turkish rulers of Syria clearly failed to appreciate the danger looming over them. Initially they were even less capable of joining forces than the Anatolian Turks. When the Crusaders besieged Yaghi Siyan of Antioch, a local coalition was formed to support him but this was defeated with ease. A more serious attempt to unify Saljuq Turkish and Arab forces from Syria, Iraq and southeastern Turkey also suffered an unexpected defeat at the hands of the Crusaders outside Antioch.

From then on Saljuq resistance evaporated for a year or so, to be replaced by shock, exhaustion and a general collapse of solidarity. Meanwhile the Crusaders regrouped and marched south out of nominally Saljuq territory into that of the Fatimid Caliphate and its allies.

FATIMID PLANS

The Fatimid government in Cairo did have a plan, but it was based upon a misinterpretation of what was actually happening. The Fatimid Grand Vizier al-Afdal had almost certainly been kept informed of the arrival and early progress of the Crusaders by the Byzantine government.

At first the Fatimid government saw the Crusade as some sort of extension of the Byzantine army and attempted to forge an alliance with its leadership against what the Fatimids regarded as their common enemy – the Saljuq Turks. These efforts continued during and after the Crusaders' conquest of Antioch. Even while the Crusaders marched through Fatimid territory in Lebanon they may still have been seen as dangerous and troublesome armed pilgrims rather than outright invaders. Perhaps their ravages could be contained if not entirely controlled? Only when the Crusaders attacked Jerusalem does it seem that the Fatimid authorities finally abandoned this delusion.

Even after the Crusaders conquered the Holy City and massacred most of its population, al-Afdal's extraordinary message to them suggests that he still hoped to reach a reasonable accommodation. Only after the defeat at Ascalon did the Fatimid government apparently realise that the Crusaders were bent on conquest. Even so they continued to regard these newcomers primarily as a buffer against the Saljuq Turks.

THE CAMPAIGN

The march by various Crusader hosts across Europe is a minor epic in itself. However, it is the events between the First Crusade leaving Constantinople (Istanbul) and its arrival at Jerusalem and subsequent defeat of the Fatimid army outside Ascalon that are the focus of this book. The political negotiations between Emperor Alexios I and the leaders of the Crusade did, however, have a direct bearing on the course of this campaign.

Byzantine political and territory claims were grudgingly accepted by the leaders of the First Crusade and the original sources indicate that all conquests were to be considered Byzantine territory. Debate continues over the interpretation of these agreements. Some Crusaders may have viewed undertakings given to the Emperor in Constantinople as mere formalities. Serious tension only emerged after taking Antioch when Alexios made it clear he regarded the agreements as binding.

Another oft-neglected aspect of the political activities in Constantinople was the correspondence between the Byzantine and Fatimid governments. Their texts do not survive but the Aleppo chronicler al-'Azimi suggests that in 1095 the Byzantine authorities informed 'the Muslims' about the arrival of the First Crusade. Alexios had no desire to 'warn' either the Anatolian Saljuqs or the Great Saljuq Sultan or his governors in Syria and clearly these later sources refer to diplomatic correspondence between Constantinople and Cairo – two capitals that shared a common enemy in the Saljuq Turks. The Fatimids probably hoped that, after the defeat of the Saljuqs, the Crusaders would take northern Syria for Byzantium while the Fatimids re-established their control in Lebanon and Palestine.

The city of Kahramanmaras seen from its Citadel. (Author's photograph)

The Byzantine military Saint Theodore portrayed on a mosaic in the Greek Monastery of Osios Loukos, made around AD1000. (Author's photograph)

The Saljuqs of Rum were soon aware of the arrival of Crusader contingents around Constantinople. On learning that the Crusaders were threatening his territory Qïlïch Arslan came to an agreement with his Danishmandid rivals and they jointly marched against the invaders.

The siege of Nicaea

Most Crusader contingents were ferried across the Bosporus from Constantinople when the weather improved early in 1097, and made camp at Pelekanon (Maltepe) on the shore of the Gulf of Izmit, within the corner of northwestern Anatolia that the Byzantines had already regained. From here most of the Crusader contingents advanced into Saljuq-held territory then followed the old Roman road from Nicomedia (Izmit) to Nicaea (Iznik). They reached Nicaea on 6 May 1097 to begin the siege. The contingents of Bohemond of Taranto, Raymond of Toulouse, Robert of Normandy and Stephen of Blois arrived over the next days and weeks. They were supported by a Byzantine contingent of around 2,000 troops under Tatikios. A second Byzantine force supplied the boats necessary to complete the siege of lakeside Nicaea. Eventually the Crusader forces outside Nicaea numbered around 4,200–4,500 cavalry and 30,000 infantry, excluding non-combatants. Meanwhile the Emperor Alexios remained at Pelekanon to supervise supplies.

On 16 May a Turkish relief army under Qïlïch Arslan and the Danishmandid *amir* had been decisively defeated. It arrived from Melitene, probably via Ancyra (Ankara) and Dorylaeum (Eskisehir). Most if not all these Turks were mounted, which enabled them to travel fast in the hope of relieving Nicaea through a sudden attack before the Crusaders established proper siege lines. Apparently the Turks attacked Raymond of Toulouse's Provençals outside the southern wall because this southern French contingent had just arrived and not yet established proper positions. The Turks would also have hoped to break into the city and reinforce the small defending garrison. But the Provençals held their ground until Godfrey of Bouillon's and Robert of Flanders' contingents rushed from the eastern side of Nicaea, striking the Turks in the flank.

The medieval Citadel of Edessa (Urfa) with the once sacred Birkit Ibrahim or 'Pool of Abraham' in the foreground. (Author's photograph)

A section of the Anglo-Norman *Bayeux Tapestry* illustrates 'Harold's ship on the way to Normandy'. More than one fleet of northern European vessels sailed into the Mediterranean and were involved in the later stages of the First Crusade. (Tapestry Museum, Bayeux)

The fighting took place in a confined area between the fortifications and some wooded hills, giving the Turks little room for manoeuvre. As a result Qïlïch Arslan's *coup de main* failed and he withdrew after heavy losses. The morale of the Crusaders now soared, as a letter from Anselm of Ribémont indicated. Apparently the victorious Christians returned 'bearing many heads fixed upon spikes and spears, offering a joyful spectacle to the people of God'. These heads were subsequently hurled into Nicaea using stone-throwing mangonels to undermine Turkish morale.

Yet the fighting continued, as Fulcher of Chartres made clear: *Our enemy shot at us and we at them, each doing his best in these encounters. With our machines we often assailed the city but because a strong wall resisted us the attack failed. Turks often perished, struck by arrows or stones, and Franks likewise ... when they slew one of our men before the wall in any way, they let down iron hooks by means of ropes and took the body up ... After stripping the corpse, they threw the body outside.*

The siege of Nicaea was not over but the defenders could not hope for another relief attempt as Qïlïch Arslan had withdrawn to gather a larger army. The arrival of more boats, sent by the Emperor Alexios, shortly following the appearance of the northern French Crusader contingent, convinced the garrison that they must surrender. Nicaea was handed over to the Byzantines while the Crusaders, ignorant of the Byzantine–Turk negotiations, made another assault upon a different section of wall on 19 June. The Crusaders were further galled by the safe conduct granted the Turkish garrison.

The western European invaders also had a large number of Muslim captives, probably from the defeat of Qïlïch Arslan on 16 May. At first this caused them problems since the ransoming of captives was not as highly developed in 11th-century western Europe as it was in the Byzantine and Islamic worlds. For their part the Crusaders were seemingly unprepared either to ransom or be ransomed, and the idea of being taken alive by the 'infidels' does not appear to have been considered. Enslaving the enemy was acceptable and many Turks captured around Nicaea were sent to

THE CRUSADERS CONVERGE ON CONSTANTINOPLE

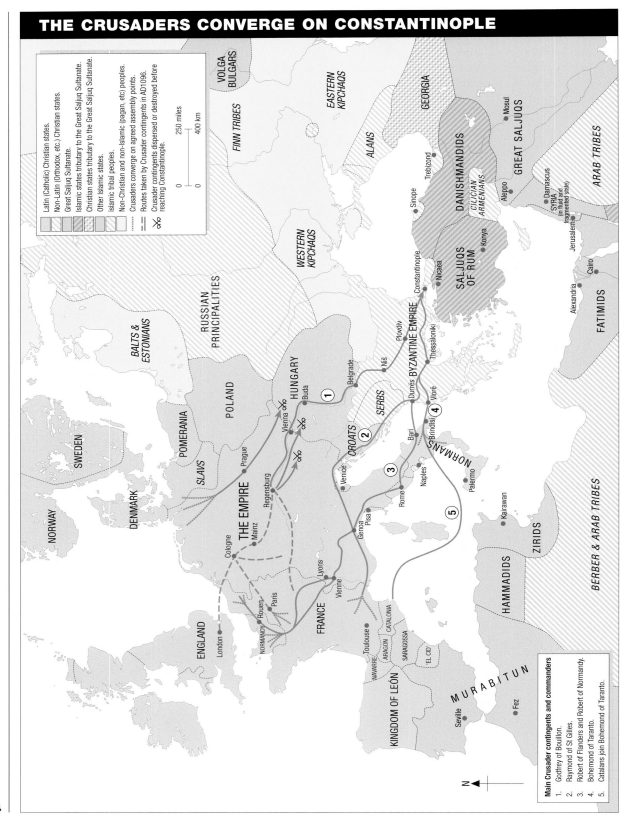

Legend:
- Latin (Catholic) Christian states.
- Non-Latin (Orthodox, etc.) Christian states.
- Great Saljuq Sultanate.
- Islamic states tributary to the Great Saljuq Sultanate.
- Christian states tributary to the Great Saljuq Sultanate.
- Other Islamic states.
- Islamic tribal peoples.
- Non-Christian and non-Islamic (pagan, etc) peoples.
- ‑ ‑ ‑ Crusaders converge on agreed assembly points.
- —— Routes taken by Crusader contingents in AD1096.
- Crusader contingents dispersed or destroyed before reaching Constantinople.

0 ___ 250 miles
0 ___ 400 km

Main Crusader contingents and commanders
1. Godfrey of Bouillon.
2. Raymond of St Gilles.
3. Robert of Flanders and Robert of Normandy.
4. Bohemond of Taranto.
5. Catalans join Bohemond of Taranto.

N

34

Constantinople for sale. One of them was a ten-year-old boy whom the Crusaders gave to the Emperor Alexios. He was renamed John Axouchos and was selected as a companion for John, the Emperor's son. John Axouchos remained devoted to the Komnenid dynasty and rose to become *Grand Domestikos* or commander of Byzantium's eastern armies.

Following the taking of Nicaea, Emperor Alexios persuaded the Crusader leadership to send envoys to the Fatimid Caliphate in Egypt. Crusader commanders were learning about the quarrels within the Islamic world but signally failed to make use of these divisions once they reached Syria. Nor did they appreciate the difficulties that lay ahead, as Stephen of Blois indicated in a letter sent to his wife in June 1097: 'I tell you my beloved, that in five weeks we shall reach Jerusalem from Nicea … unless Antioch stands in our way.'

During the trek across Anatolia a Byzantine force of some 2,000 men commanded by Tatikios marched in the vanguard because it included guides and, perhaps, interpreters. This placed Tatikios close to Bohemond of Taranto whose men, along with those of Robert of Normandy, headed the line of march. The army should not, perhaps, be described as a column since there were substantial gaps between various contingents – a fact that would have a major impact on their next battle.

The Crusaders now followed a route close to the foothills of the western and southern Anatolian mountains, keeping the arid Anatolian high plateau on their left flank. This took them through a bleak region of salt-lakes and dried salt-flats between the cities of Amorium (Afyon), Baris (Isparta) and Iconium (Konya). Before this, however, the Crusaders faced another serious challenge from Qïlich Arslan and his allies at the misnamed battle of Dorylaeum.

An armed but unarmoured warrior on a southern French carved capital dating from the start of the 12th century. (*In situ* Cloisters of the Abbey of St Pierre, Moissac; author's photograph)

THE AMBUSH AT DORYLAEUM

A recent study of the Crusaders' route prior to the battle seems to have solved the problems of interpretation that had dogged this part of the First Crusade[2] It suggests that the Crusader host used a road further west than historians had previously assumed, thus avoiding the narrow and potentially dangerous lower gorges of the Kara Su river and following an old Roman road across the Ahl mountains. This brought the Crusaders and their guides down the valley of the river Murat before following the Kara Su valley until it was joined by the small river Nane and turned abruptly westward.

The new proposed site of the battlefield is 56 kilometres west of Eskisehir (ancient Dorylaeum) but every aspect fits the written descriptions of the battle. It is also clear that the front of the Crusader line of march was attacked with little warning by an enemy hidden behind hills. Some Turks must surely have been shadowing the Crusaders and the information that they sent to Qïlich Arslan would have enabled him to select a battlefield offering advantages to the Turks' traditional tactics.

The leading division or vanguard of the Crusader army, consisting of the Byzantine contingent under Tatikios plus those of Bohemond of

Taranto, Stephen of Blois and Robert of Flanders, were about five kilometres ahead of the second division and rearguard. A small shadowing force of Turkish cavalry may have adopted a position on low hills facing the Kara Su valley where it joined the broader valley of the Nane Dere. Meanwhile the main Turkish army under Qïlïch Arslan had formed up across the Nane valley, blocking the invaders' advance towards Dorylaeum but out of sight until the Crusaders emerged from the Kara Su valley. The Turkish array probably consisted of their traditional centre and two wings.

As the Crusader vanguard reached the junction of the Kara Su and Nane rivers, they would have seen the main Turkish army on their right. The Crusaders would presumably have been aware of any Turkish 'shadowing force' on the hills. It was Bohemond of Taranto who ordered the infantry to make a defensive camp, partially protected by a 'flowery meadow' or marsh that still exists. Bohemond also ordered the cavalry to form up protecting the infantry as they established a defensive position. The main Turkish force now attacked the Crusader cavalry, forcing it back against infantry defending the camp's perimeter. The sources make it very clear that the Turkish harassing archery tactics initially confused the Crusaders. Fulcher of Chartres described the situation vividly: *The Turks crept up, howling loudly and shooting a shower of arrows. Stunned and almost dead, and with many wounded, we immediately fled. And it was no wonder, for such warfare was new to us all.*

The remains of the Tutah Mosque in Aleppo, dating from the late 11th century. (Author's photograph)

The *Gesta Francorum* similarly described Turks 'Skirmishing, throwing darts and javelins and shooting arrows from an astonishing range'. Meanwhile part of the Turkish force probably swung left to find and attack the rest of the Crusader army that, if the scouts had been doing their duty, Qïlïch Arslan must surely have known existed. However, this part of the Turkish army attacked stragglers between the widely separated van and second or rear divisions of the Crusader column, maybe mistaking them for the remainder of the Crusader host.

The survivors probably fled to the Crusader contingents under Godfrey of Bouillon and Raymond of Toulouse, which may have been as much as five kilometres behind the vanguard. Perhaps as a result of movement by Godfrey of Bouillon's contingent, the separated Turkish left wing presumably fell back to rejoin the main Turkish force but may have remained ignorant of the presence of a third Crusader contingent – the rearguard under Raymond of Toulouse. Turkish cavalry of a presumed 'shadowing force' may have meanwhile attacked and penetrated the other side of the Crusader camp.

When Godfrey of Bouillon's division reached the battlefield they probably formed up on the right of Bohemond of Taranto, perhaps obliging the Turkish main force to pull back and face slightly to their left. More significantly Raymond of Toulouse's division, having probably been

Two infantrymen armed with long-hafted war-axes on a capital carved very early in the 12th century. (*In situ* Cloisters of the Abbey of St Pierre, Moissac; author's photograph)

Part of the remains of the fortified southeastern walls of Antioch seen from the inside. (author's photograph)

at the rear of the Crusader column, presumably entered the valley of the river Nane over the shoulder of the hill. This took them though a series of drumlins or oval alluvial mounds formed by seasonal floodwater. These did not form a serious obstacle but might have obscured the movements of Raymond's troops. Certainly Raymond charged into the Turkish flank quite unexpectedly. Qïlïch Arslan's army reeled and fled. The Crusaders had won another decisive victory.

The Turkish defeats outside Nicaea and at the battle of Dorylaeum resulted from tactical errors by Qïlïch Arslan and the great numerical superiority of the Crusaders. The Frankish victory at Dorylaeum was also

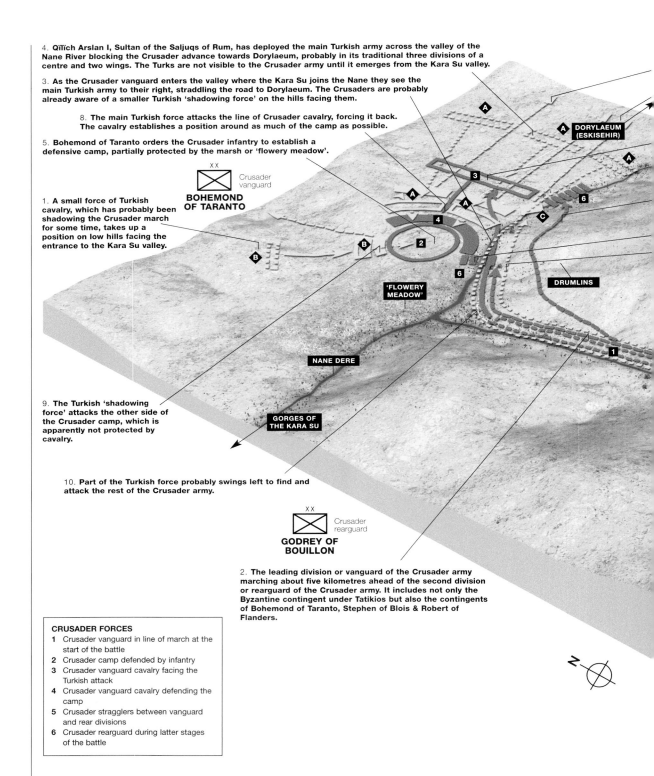

4. Qïlïch Arslan I, Sultan of the Saljuqs of Rum, has deployed the main Turkish army across the valley of the Nane River blocking the Crusader advance towards Dorylaeum, probably in its traditional three divisions of a centre and two wings. The Turks are not visible to the Crusader army until it emerges from the Kara Su valley.

3. As the Crusader vanguard enters the valley where the Kara Su joins the Nane they see the main Turkish army to their right, straddling the road to Dorylaeum. The Crusaders are probably already aware of a smaller Turkish 'shadowing force' on the hills facing them.

8. The main Turkish force attacks the line of Crusader cavalry, forcing it back. The cavalry establishes a position around as much of the camp as possible.

5. Bohemond of Taranto orders the Crusader infantry to establish a defensive camp, partially protected by the marsh or 'flowery meadow'.

BOHEMOND OF TARANTO
Crusader vanguard

1. A small force of Turkish cavalry, which has probably been shadowing the Crusader march for some time, takes up a position on low hills facing the entrance to the Kara Su valley.

9. The Turkish 'shadowing force' attacks the other side of the Crusader camp, which is apparently not protected by cavalry.

10. Part of the Turkish force probably swings left to find and attack the rest of the Crusader army.

GODREY OF BOUILLON
Crusader rearguard

2. The leading division or vanguard of the Crusader army marching about five kilometres ahead of the second division or rearguard of the Crusader army. It includes not only the Byzantine contingent under Tatikios but also the contingents of Bohemond of Taranto, Stephen of Blois & Robert of Flanders.

DORYLAEUM (ESKISEHIR)

'FLOWERY MEADOW'

DRUMLINS

NANE DERE

GORGES OF THE KARA SU

CRUSADER FORCES
1 Crusader vanguard in line of march at the start of the battle
2 Crusader camp defended by infantry
3 Crusader vanguard cavalry facing the Turkish attack
4 Crusader vanguard cavalry defending the camp
5 Crusader stragglers between vanguard and rear divisions
6 Crusader rearguard during latter stages of the battle

THE BATTLE OF DORYLAEUM

1 July 1097, viewed from the southwest. The Crusader army (following the erratic course of the Kara Su River and actually marching north at this moment) is ambushed by a combined Saljuq/Danishmandid army under Qïlïlich Arslan.

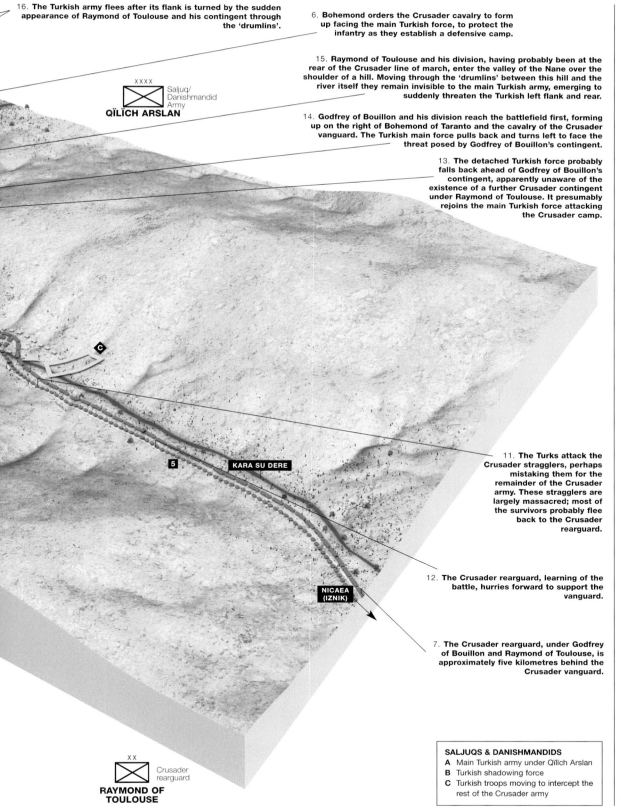

16. The Turkish army flees after its flank is turned by the sudden appearance of Raymond of Toulouse and his contingent through the 'drumlins'.

6. Bohemond orders the Crusader cavalry to form up facing the main Turkish force, to protect the infantry as they establish a defensive camp.

15. Raymond of Toulouse and his division, having probably been at the rear of the Crusader line of march, enter the valley of the Nane over the shoulder of a hill. Moving through the 'drumlins' between this hill and the river itself they remain invisible to the main Turkish army, emerging to suddenly threaten the Turkish left flank and rear.

14. Godfrey of Bouillon and his division reach the battlefield first, forming up on the right of Bohemond of Taranto and the cavalry of the Crusader vanguard. The Turkish main force pulls back and turns left to face the threat posed by Godfrey of Bouillon's contingent.

13. The detached Turkish force probably falls back ahead of Godfrey of Bouillon's contingent, apparently unaware of the existence of a further Crusader contingent under Raymond of Toulouse. It presumably rejoins the main Turkish force attacking the Crusader camp.

XXXX
Saljuq/
Danishmandid
Army
QÏLÏCH ARSLAN

C

5   **KARA SU DERE**

11. The Turks attack the Crusader stragglers, perhaps mistaking them for the remainder of the Crusader army. These stragglers are largely massacred; most of the survivors probably flee back to the Crusader rearguard.

12. The Crusader rearguard, learning of the battle, hurries forward to support the vanguard.

NICAEA (IZNIK)

7. The Crusader rearguard, under Godfrey of Bouillon and Raymond of Toulouse, is approximately five kilometres behind the Crusader vanguard.

XX
Crusader
rearguard
RAYMOND OF TOULOUSE

SALJUQS & DANISHMANDIDS
A Main Turkish army under Qïlïch Arslan
B Turkish shadowing force
C Turkish troops moving to intercept the rest of the Crusader army

The Crusaders' capture of Antioch as shown in the early 18th-century drawing of the lost stained-glass windows of St Denis in Paris. The tower at the top represents the Citadel, which did not fall until after the defeat of Kür-Bugha's relieving army.

achieved by an effective combination of cavalry and foot soldiers, knights and infantry archers or crossbowmen. The *Gesta Francorum* was, however, full of praise for the Turks: *Whoever will be wise or learned enough to dare to describe the valour, skill, and fortitude of the Turks ... I shall speak the truth, which no one will dare deny. Certainly, if they had ever been firm in the faith of Christ and holy Christianity ... no one could have found more powerful, braver or more skilful fighters than they.*

Raymond d'Aguilers indicates that many Turks were taken captive after the battle and some converted to Christianity. This was probably why the anonymous author of the *Gesta Francorum* was able to include detailed though garbled information about Qïlïch Arslan's army, whose ranks supposedly included *Agulani* and *Publicani*. The former were clearly *ghulams* or elite troops of slave-recruited origin, while the latter were probably *Paulicians*, members of a religious group that had long sought refuge from Christian persecution in eastern Anatolia.

The Crusader host now continued its march south through the 'bad lands'. The Danishmandid army seems to have returned to its own territory after Dorylaeum but Qïlïch Arslan probably withdrew ahead of the advancing Crusaders. There seems to have been little resistance during this part of the Crusader march, the Greek Christian inhabitants of the towns and cities opening their gates after small local Turkish garrisons withdrew.

The Crusaders reached Iconium (Konya) in mid-August and received a friendly reception but they neither occupied this city nor handed it over to a Byzantine garrison. The Crusaders may have considered Iconium untenable. Certainly Qïlïch Arslan selected it as his new capital once the

One of the halls in the ruined Citadel overlooking Antioch. (Frederick Nicolle photograph)

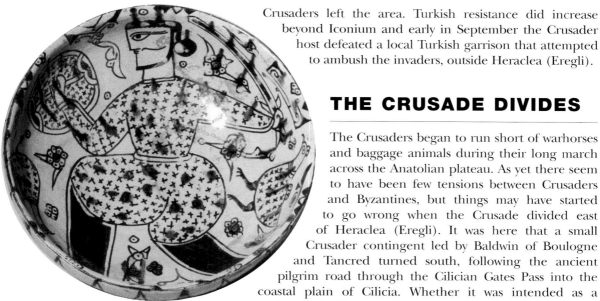

A dismounted Islamic cavalryman armed with a sword and small round shield but still wearing riding boots, on a 10th- or 11th-century ceramic plate from Nishapur. (Private collection)

Crusaders left the area. Turkish resistance did increase beyond Iconium and early in September the Crusader host defeated a local Turkish garrison that attempted to ambush the invaders, outside Heraclea (Eregli).

THE CRUSADE DIVIDES

The Crusaders began to run short of warhorses and baggage animals during their long march across the Anatolian plateau. As yet there seem to have been few tensions between Crusaders and Byzantines, but things may have started to go wrong when the Crusade divided east of Heraclea (Eregli). It was here that a small Crusader contingent led by Baldwin of Boulogne and Tancred turned south, following the ancient pilgrim road through the Cilician Gates Pass into the coastal plain of Cilicia. Whether it was intended as a reconnaissance in force or diversion, or was merely a matter of 'land grabbing' by two relatively junior leaders is unclear. The bulk of the Crusader host, plus the Byzantine contingent under Tatikios, headed northeast into Cappadocia.

There were several possible reasons for this apparent diversion. Perhaps the Crusaders feared an ambush in the Cilician Gates, which had formed an easily defensible frontier between the Byzantine Empire and the Islamic states for three centuries. The pass itself was, however, easier than those the bulk of the Crusaders eventually used between Caesarea Mazacha (Kayseri) and Marash (Kahramanmaras), which were more likely to be closed by winter snow.

In fact the reasons were probably political and served Byzantine rather than Crusader interests. Autonomous Armenian princes still survived in the eastern Taurus and Soganli mountains while the Byzantines had reasonable hopes of regaining the still largely Armenian Christian cities of eastern Cappadocia. On the other hand Armenian princes further west in the Taurus mountains were generally anti-Byzantine and some Crusader leaders already had contacts with various Armenian leaders.

The local Turkish rulers did not give up without a fight and in mid-September, outside a place called Augustopolis the Crusaders defeated the army of a leader named Hasan or Baldaji, who had once been a rival to Qïlïch Arslan for authority over the Saljuq Sultanate of Rum. The *Gesta Francorum* records the taking of what was probably Pinarbasi in the fertile Zamanti valley: *Going out of Cappadocia we came to a certain very beautiful and exceedingly fruitful city which the Turks had besieged for three weeks before our arrival but had not conquered. Immediately upon our arrival there it straightway surrendered into our hands with great pleasure. A certain knight whose name was Peter of Aups* [a western mercenary in Byzantine service] *begged ... to defend it in fealty to God, the Holy Sepulchre, the seigneurs and the Emperor. They granted it to him freely ...*

Byzantine garrisons were left in several places as the Crusader host advanced, including Caesarea Mazacha (Kayseri) and Coxon (Göksun), considerably reducing the strength of Tatikios' corps. Even with local

The interior of the church built around the grotto of St Peter in the hills just east of Antioch. (Author's photograph)

THE BATTLE OF DORYLAEUM (pages 42–43)

The main Turkish army under Qïlïch Arslan I (1), ruler of the Sultanate of Rum in Anatolia, had formed up across the valley of the Nane Dere. Here it blocked the Crusader horde's advance towards the city of Dorylaeum but was also out of sight of the enemy until the latter emerged from the Kara Su valley. The Turks were probably in their traditional three divisions consisting of a centre and two wings. As the Crusader vanguard reached the point where the Kara Su and Nane streams joined, they would have seen the main Turkish army to their right, probably straddling the road to Dorylaeum. While Bohemond of Taranto ordered the Crusader infantry to erect a defensive camp, partially protected by a marsh or 'flowery meadow', the Crusader cavalry formed up facing Qïlïch Arslan's troops. At this point the main Turkish force attacked the line of Crusader cavalry, forcing it back to the defensive camp. The sources clearly state that the Crusaders were initially confused by the Turks' harassing archery tactics, which is why they retreated like huddled masses in an arrow storm. Fulcher of Chartres described the situation vividly; 'The Turks crept up, howling loudly and shooting a shower of arrows. Stunned and almost dead, and with many wounded, we immediately fled. And it was no wonder, for such warfare was new to us all'. The *Gesta Francorum* similarly described Turks, 'Skirmishing, throwing darts and javelins and shooting arrows from an astonishing range'. In this picture the only Turkish archery equipment visible is Qïlïch Arslan's own quiver (2), though he would also have had a bowcase over his left thigh. Battlefield control was vital for such sophisticated tactics and here the Turks could use both Central Asian and long-established Middle Eastern systems. The former included war-drums played by professional military musicians, usually riding mules (3) while the latter included large animals such as camels carrying banners as mobile rallying points (4). However, before the Turkish commander's élite armoured *ghulam* cavalry (7) could penetrate the Crusader line they were themselves unexpectedly attacked in the flank by a second Crusader force and forced to retreat in disorder. The armies of Qïlïch Arslan and his Danishmandid Turkish ally clearly included a great variety of troops. These ranged from relatively lightly armoured tribesmen (5), through professional freeborn soldiers who would have used a variety of equipment (6) to the heavily armoured elite of slave-recruited *ghulams* (7). Apart from abundant armour of mail and lamellar construction, the status of the *ghulams* would almost certainly have been indicated by distinctive and highly decorated military belts as well as gilded fittings on the swords (8). On the other hand archaeological discoveries show that highly decorated and sometimes gilded horse-harness was popular amongst almost all ranks (9). (Christa Hook)

Armenian assistance the army suffered terrible hardship and numerous casualties crossing the mountains, while the losses of warhorses and baggage animals was catastrophic. Many fighting men offered to sell military equipment for money to buy food while others just threw their kit away because it was too heavy without a beast of burden. The appearance of a comet also had a big impact on hungry, exhausted but religiously excited people. Meanwhile various latecomers caught up with the Crusader host as it made its way across Anatolia. The local Armenians of Marash did, however, welcome the Crusaders, who in turn left a pro-Byzantine Armenian lord named Tatoul in control before pressing on. A friendly Marash would prove a strategic advantage not only in the siege of Antioch, but also in the future history of the Crusader states. Baldwin of Boulogne and his followers also crossed the main army's line of march at Marash.

A lack of resistance in these mountains enabled the Crusaders to split their forces on several occasions and a Provençal garrison was installed at Ariha, deep within northern Syria. This indicated how unprepared the local Islamic forces were and may cast doubt on the belief that the Crusaders had only 700–1,000 warhorses.

Meanwhile the Crusader force that had invaded Cilicia had an easier time and found a number of Flemish 'pirate' ships moored near Tarsus. They were commanded by Guynemer of Boulogne, who claimed to be a vassal of Count Eustace of Boulogne and had supposedly been operating in the northeastern Mediterranean for eight years. Some historians consider this Flemish fleet to have formed part of an Anglo-Saxon fleet in Byzantine service that was in the area by March 1098. Although direct navigation between the Byzantine Empire and northern Europe via the Straits of Gibraltar was unusual, it did take place. The ships that Guynemer of Boulogne and the Anglo-Saxon refugees under Edgar

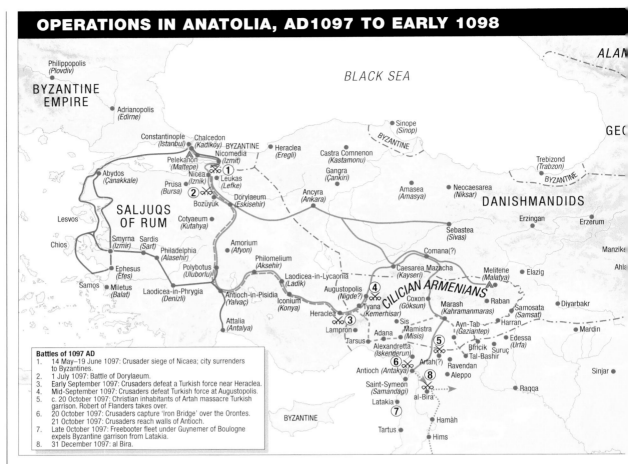

Battles of 1097 AD
1. 14 May–19 June 1097: Crusader siege of Nicaea; city surrenders to Byzantines.
2. 1 July 1097: Battle of Dorylaeum.
3. Early September 1097: Crusaders defeat a Turkish force near Heraclea.
4. Mid-September 1097: Crusaders defeat Turkish force at Augustopolis.
5. c. 20 October 1097: Christian inhabitants of Artah massacre Turkish garrison. Robert of Flanders takes over.
6. 20 October 1097: Crusaders capture 'Iron Bridge' over the Orontes.
   21 October 1097: Crusaders reach walls of Antioch.
7. Late October 1097: Freebooter fleet under Guynemer of Boulogne expels Byzantine garrison from Latakia.
8. 31 December 1097: al Bira.

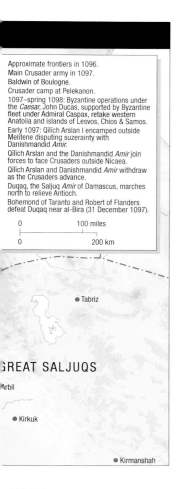

Approximate frontiers in 1096.
Main Crusader army in 1097.
Baldwin of Boulogne.
Crusader camp at Pelekanon.
1097–spring 1098: Byzantine operations under the *Caesar*, John Ducas, supported by Byzantine fleet under Admiral Caspax, retake western Anatolia and islands of Lesvos, Chios & Samos.
Early 1097: Qïlïch Arslan I encamped outside Melitene disputing suzerainty with Danishmandid *Amir*.
Qïlïch Arslan and the Danishmandid *Amir* join forces to face Crusaders outside Nicaea.
Qïlïch Arslan and Danishmandid *Amir* withdraw as the Crusaders advance.
Duqaq, the Saljuq *Amir* of Damascus, marches north to relieve Antioch.
Bohemond of Taranto and Robert of Flanders defeat Duqaq near al-Bira (31 December 1097).

0   100 miles
0   200 km

GREAT SALJUQS

Arbil

Kirkuk

Kirmanshah

Tabriz

LEFT **The late Byzantine and early medieval Islamic ruins of the largely abandoned city of al-Bira in northwestern Syria. (Author's photograph)**

ABOVE, RIGHT **An archer using a southern Italian form of probably composite bow, on a late 11th-century carved capital. (*In situ* Church of San Giovanni, Ravello; Ian Peirce photograph)**

Atheling sailed from the English Channel to the eastern Mediterranean were probably not warships but would have been of the Scandinavian *knörr* or English *buss* type. Any warships present are likely to have been Byzantine galleys.

Following its operations in Cilicia, the smaller Crusader force headed east; Tancred and his followers reaching Mamistra (Misis) while Baldwin of Boulogne pressed on to Edessa (Urfa) having received a request for help from one of its rival Armenian factions. His small force evaded interception by a Saljuq garrison from Samosate (Samsat) and arrived on 20 February 1098. The existing ruler of Edessa, T'oros (Theodore) Kurbalat son of Hethoum, had succeeded the Byzantine-Armenian ruler Philaretus, who had for several years also ruled Antioch. The faction that invited Baldwin seems to have opposed T'oros and it was presumably with its help that he overthrew T'oros in March 1098, to become the first Crusader Count of Edessa.

Byzantines and Muslims

The First Crusade was part of a broader campaign. While the Crusaders marched towards Syria, the Emperor Alexios undertook separate operations to regain western Anatolia from the Saljuqs and other Turks.

An army under John Doukas disembarked at Abydos near modern Çanakkale and marched down the coast to retake Smyrna (Izmir) from the *amir* Çaka's successors. It was supported by a Byzantine fleet under Admiral Caspax that expelled small Turkish garrisons from Lesvos, Chios and Samos. Smyrna's fortifications were strengthened while Byzantine forces converged on Ephesus (Efes). Next a Byzantine army led by the Emperor himself headed inland to take Sardis (Sart), Philadelphia (Alasehir) and Laodicea (Denizli). From here they crossed the mountains to the region through which the Crusaders had passed the previous summer.

The Emperor now established his headquarters at Philomelium (Aksehir) while Qïlïch Arslan may have retaken Iconium. But Alexios was unsure what the Saljuqs would do next. Might they challenge his reconquests, support the Saljuq garrison in Antioch, or merely hold **47**

Soldier in a segmented or fluted helmet or hat, carrying a long-hafted mace and leading a horse, on an 11th- or early 12th-century carved wooden panel from Fatimid Egypt. (Musée du Louvre, Paris)

Iconium, their future capital? Instead the rivalry between the Saljuqs of Rum and the Danishmandids re-ignited almost as soon as the Crusaders had left, once again focusing on domination over Melitene (Malatya).

Meanwhile Alexios organised supplies for the Crusaders now besieging Antioch. These went by sea as the returning Turks had apparently severed the overland link between the Byzantines at Philomelium and the Crusaders around Antioch. In fact Turkish raiders killed some belated Danish Crusaders near Philomelium.

Having withdrawn his remaining troops from the Crusader siege of Antioch early in February 1098, Tatikios made his way back by sea to rejoin his Emperor at Philomelium. There he was sent to command a force sent against a Pisan fleet that had attacked Byzantine shipping. Another Byzantine officer named Landulph, appears to have commanded the Byzantine ships. The Pisans were actually on their way to join the Crusaders but were defeated by Tatikios and Landulph who pursued them to the Syrian coast where the Pisans offered their services to Bohemond of Taranto.

Alexios was still at Philomelium when Stephen of Blois arrived in June 1098, having abandoned the siege of Antioch in despair. Stephen's belief that the Crusader army must now have been destroyed persuaded Alexios to adopt a defensive posture in case of a Saljuq counterattack. Various Crusaders who missed the first contingents were also turned back by Alexios, though some pressed on in the hope, as they said, 'of finding the bodies of their friends'. Eventually the Emperor Alexios abandoned Philomelium, resettling its population in the Balkans, pulling back to a defensible frontier in the mountains while his men laid waste the area to create a no man's land. This supposed 'abandonment' of the Crusaders by the Emperor Alexios proved a turning point and mutual mistrust steadily increased.

In Syria, meanwhile, local Saljuq and other governors were embroiled in petty squabbles. In 1096 Ridwan of Aleppo and his *atabeg* or guardian, Janah al-Dawla, took the small city of Ma'arat al-Nu'man from Yaghi Siyan of Antioch. Later that year Janah al-Dawla joined Ridwan and Sökmen Ibn Artuk of Diyarbakr, who, with his brother Il-Ghazi, also ruled Jerusalem, in an attack on Sökmen's supposed overlord, Duqaq of Damascus. But Janah al-Dawla withdrew before the campaign ended. Yaghi Siyan of Antioch now tried to promote discord between Ridwan and Janah al-Dawla. In 1097 Duqaq of Damascus invaded Aleppo's territory and this time Janah al-Dawla left Ridwan and Sökmen to face him alone. Ridwan was victorious in a clash near Qinnisrin, leading Janah al-Dawla to flee with his wife – Ridwan's mother – and establish himself as the independent ruler of Hims. Yaghi Siyan now formed an alliance with Ridwan and gave his daughter in marriage to the ruler of Aleppo. The new allies then teamed up with

Sökmen Ibn Artuk and headed for Hims, which they intended to take from Janah al-Dawla before marching against Damascus. Instead of attacking Damascus, however, the three allies moved against Arab-ruled Shayzar, perhaps intending to attack Hims and Damascus afterwards.

A few weeks after beginning their siege of Shayzar, the allies learned of the approaching Crusader horde. Yaghi Siyan promptly hurried back to Antioch but Ridwan and Sökmen refused to accompany him. Instead they returned to their own power-bases to observe events.

THE SIEGE OF ANTIOCH

As soon as the Crusaders reached Yaghi Siyan's territory in October 1097 he sent his son with an urgent appeal for help to other Islamic rulers. However, the results were disappointing and there was the problem of Antioch's largely Christian population. According to Ibn al-Athir: *When Yaghi Siyan … heard of their* [the Crusaders'] *approach he was not sure how the Christian people of the city would react, so he made the Muslims go outside the city to dig trenches, and the next day he sent the Christians out to continue the task. When they were ready to return home at the end of the day he refused to allow them in. 'Antioch is yours,' he said, 'but you will have to leave it to me until I see what happens between us and the Franks.' 'Who will protect our children and our wives?' they said. 'I shall look after them for you.' So they resigned themselves to their fate, and lived in the Frankish camp for nine months while the city was under siege.*

In reality Yaghi Siyan only expelled some of the Christian leadership and he kept his word by protecting their families. In contrast, when the Crusade reached Baghras the Christian inhabitants killed many of the Turkish garrison and expelled the rest, as did the inhabitants of 'Artah.

Christian domination of the seas between Anatolia, Cyprus and northern Syria was vital to the Crusader siege of Antioch. Byzantine naval

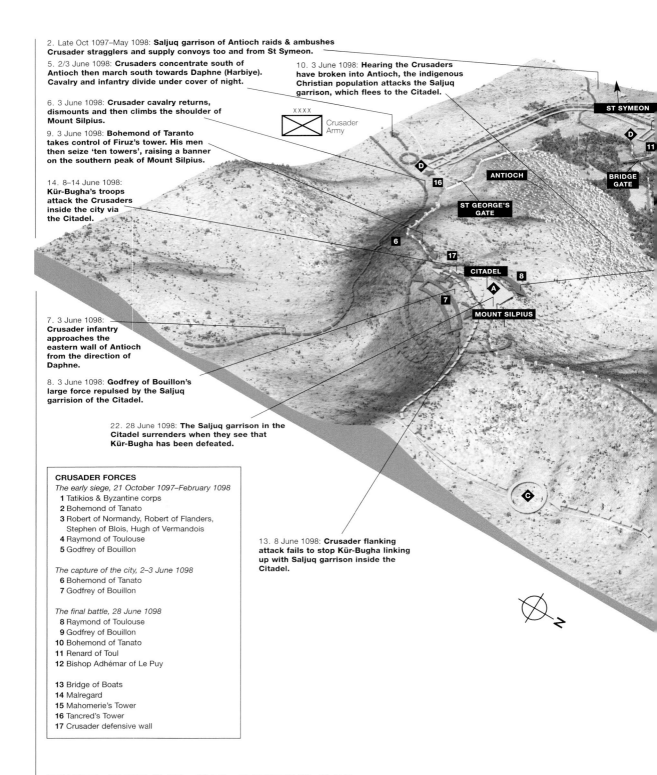

2. Late Oct 1097–May 1098: Saljuq garrison of Antioch raids & ambushes Crusader stragglers and supply convoys too and from St Symeon.

5. 2/3 June 1098: Crusaders concentrate south of Antioch then march south towards Daphne (Harbiye). Cavalry and infantry divide under cover of night.

10. 3 June 1098: Hearing the Crusaders have broken into Antioch, the indigenous Christian population attacks the Saljuq garrison, which flees to the Citadel.

6. 3 June 1098: Crusader cavalry returns, dismounts and then climbs the shoulder of Mount Silpius.

9. 3 June 1098: Bohemond of Taranto takes control of Firuz's tower. His men then seize 'ten towers', raising a banner on the southern peak of Mount Silpius.

14. 8–14 June 1098: Kür-Bugha's troops attack the Crusaders inside the city via the Citadel.

XXXX
Crusader Army

ST SYMEON

D

11

ANTIOCH

BRIDGE GATE

D

16

ST GEORGE'S GATE

6

17

CITADEL

8

A

7

MOUNT SILPIUS

7. 3 June 1098: Crusader infantry approaches the eastern wall of Antioch from the direction of Daphne.

8. 3 June 1098: Godfrey of Bouillon's large force repulsed by the Saljuq garrision of the Citadel.

22. 28 June 1098: The Saljuq garrison in the Citadel surrenders when they see that Kür-Bugha has been defeated.

C

CRUSADER FORCES
The early siege, 21 October 1097–February 1098
  1 Tatikios & Byzantine corps
  2 Bohemond of Tanato
  3 Robert of Normandy, Robert of Flanders, Stephen of Blois, Hugh of Vermandois
  4 Raymond of Toulouse
  5 Godfrey of Bouillon

The capture of the city, 2–3 June 1098
  6 Bohemond of Tanato
  7 Godfrey of Bouillon

The final battle, 28 June 1098
  8 Raymond of Toulouse
  9 Godfrey of Bouillon
  10 Bohemond of Tanato
  11 Renard of Toul
  12 Bishop Adhémar of Le Puy

  13 Bridge of Boats
  14 Malregard
  15 Mahomerie's Tower
  16 Tancred's Tower
  17 Crusader defensive wall

13. 8 June 1098: Crusader flanking attack fails to stop Kür-Bugha linking up with Saljuq garrison inside the Citadel.

N

THE SIEGE OF ANTIOCH

October 1097–June 1098, viewed from the northeast, showing the Crusader siege of Antioch and the assault and capture of the city. Kür-Bugha's army marches to the relief of the Saljuq garrison holding out in the citadel, but is defeated by the Crusaders outside the city.

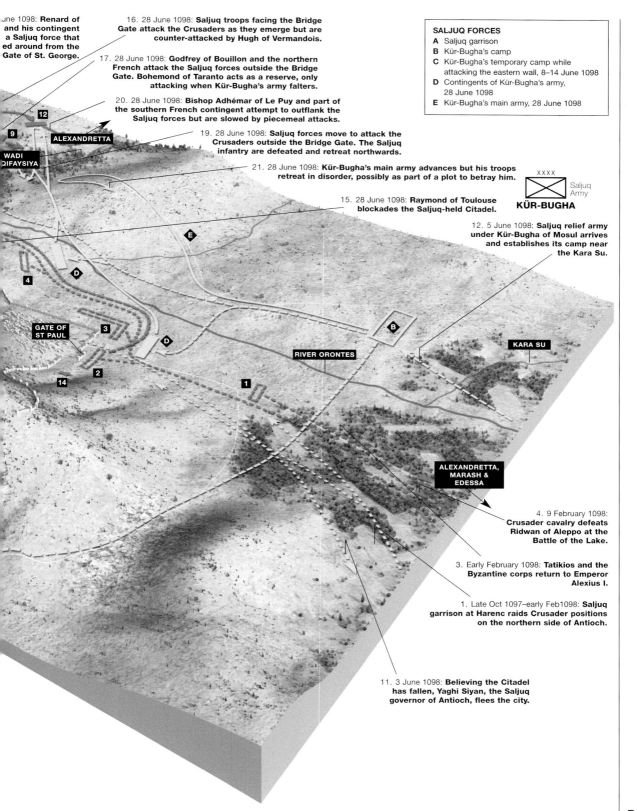

une 1098: **Renard of
and his contingent
a Saljuq force that
ed around from the
Gate of St. George.**

16. 28 June 1098: **Saljuq troops facing the Bridge
Gate attack the Crusaders as they emerge but are
counter-attacked by Hugh of Vermandois.**

17. 28 June 1098: **Godfrey of Bouillon and the northern
French attack the Saljuq forces outside the Bridge
Gate. Bohemond of Taranto acts as a reserve, only
attacking when Kür-Bugha's army falters.**

20. 28 June 1098: **Bishop Adhémar of Le Puy and part of
the southern French contingent attempt to outflank the
Saljuq forces but are slowed by piecemeal attacks.**

19. 28 June 1098: **Saljuq forces move to attack the
Crusaders outside the Bridge Gate. The Saljuq
infantry are defeated and retreat northwards.**

21. 28 June 1098: **Kür-Bugha's main army advances but his troops
retreat in disorder, possibly as part of a plot to betray him.**

15. 28 June 1098: **Raymond of Toulouse
blockades the Saljuq-held Citadel.**

12. 5 June 1098: **Saljuq relief army
under Kür-Bugha of Mosul arrives
and establishes its camp near
the Kara Su.**

SALJUQ FORCES
A   Saljuq garrison
B   Kür-Bugha's camp
C   Kür-Bugha's temporary camp while
    attacking the eastern wall, 8–14 June 1098
D   Contingents of Kür-Bugha's army,
    28 June 1098
E   Kür-Bugha's main army, 28 June 1098

XXXX
Saljuq
Army
KÜR-BUGHA

ALEXANDRETTA
**WADI
QIFAYSIYA**
12
9

E
4
D
**GATE OF
ST PAUL**
3
D
2
14
1
RIVER ORONTES
B
KARA SU

**ALEXANDRETTA,
MARASH &
EDESSA**

4. 9 February 1098:
**Crusader cavalry defeats
Ridwan of Aleppo at the
Battle of the Lake.**

3. Early February 1098: **Tatikios and the
Byzantine corps return to Emperor
Alexius I.**

1. Late Oct 1097–early Feb1098: **Saljuq
garrison at Harenc raids Crusader positions
on the northern side of Antioch.**

11. 3 June 1098: **Believing the Citadel
has fallen, Yaghi Siyan, the Saljuq
governor of Antioch, flees the city.**

51

support had been agreed back in Constantinople and the Byzantine island of Cyprus sent regular ships full of supplies. But the invaders also needed ports, like Saint-Symeon (Samandag) and Latakia. The Chronicler Kamal al-Din stated that Christian ships from Cyprus, probably an Anglo-Saxon fleet in Byzantine service, took Latakia as early as 19 August 1097. It seems that these ships also seized Saint-Symeon. Guynemer of Boulogne then took over Latakia in late October 1097, expelling any Byzantine garrison, while Guynemer's ally Tancred advanced through the northerly port of Alexandretta (Iskenderun) to rejoin the Crusader army as the latter established siege lines around Antioch.

On 15 July 1097 a fleet of 12 galleys and one larger *sandanum* transport left Genoa with armed men and equipment to support the Crusade. It reached Saint-Symeon in just over four months. These Genoese galleys were the only warships available to the Crusaders until after the fall of Jerusalem. In late November and December the Crusaders also built a bridge of boats across the river Orontes while a counter-castle known as 'Malregard' was erected on the left flank of the Crusader siege-lines as a defence against raids by the Saljuq garrison in the castle of Harenc (Harim). An earlier attempt to capture Harenc had failed.

At the start of the siege Crusader morale was very high. In another letter home to his wife, Stephen of Blois maintained that a Fatimid delegation had already made peace and, like many others, he expected a quick victory. Nor was Stephen concerned about the army's lack of supplies for the forthcoming winter. In a letter written outside Antioch in January 1098, the exiled Byzantine Patriarch of Jerusalem did call for reinforcement from Europe, but claimed that the Crusaders had already won five battles, taken 40 cities and 200 fortresses, and numbered 100,000 armoured men 'not counting the common throng'. The army was indeed large, but not that large.

In reality the following winter was harsh. Casualties from the siege were probably light but large numbers of people fell sick and many died. Sickness raised the proportion of non-combatants while losses of horses and equipment in Anatolia had rendered many men 'ineffective'. By the same process many of the so-called 'poor' became genuinely destitute

Representations of Norman knights charging the Anglo-Saxons during the battle of Hastings, on the *Bayeux Tapestry*. It clearly shows lances being used both overarm and in the couched manner. (Tapestry Museum, Bayeux)

during the siege of Antioch. Large numbers starved to death and it was during this difficult period that the *Tafurs* emerged as a well-organised band of 'poor' led by a lordless Norman knight. Men and women went on foraging expeditions around Antioch but they, like the supply convoys making their way from the ports to the besiegers, needed troops to protect them from Islamic units operating from or around Antioch.

Meanwhile the situation within Antioch eased and plenty of supplies apparently got into the city. Large as the Crusader host was, it could not impose a complete blockade on Antioch and access and egress were still possible via the eastern walls and Citadel. Certainly the Saljuq garrison could come out of the city to harass Crusader siege-lines and intercept supply convoys from Saint-Symeon and Alexandretta.

It was the besiegers who suffered shortages, including a lack of horses. Raymond of Toulouse, being wealthier and better organised than the northern leaders, contributed 500 marks to purchase remounts for many knights. Where these horses came from is unclear. Perhaps they were bought from local Christians, or perhaps the Byzantines shipped them from Cyprus. The besiegers were similarly short of timber to build counter-fortifications, which was why Tancred's unsuccessful observation post facing the Gate of St George was made of rubble and earth. A more substantial fortification called Tancred's Tower was later constructed in April 1098.

Relations with the Byzantines declined, though anti-Byzantine feeling was more widespread amongst the rank-and-file than amongst the Crusader leadership. Tatikios had in fact suggested pressing the siege more closely to stop the garrison from coming in and out so easily, but the Crusader leaders maintained that this would make them vulnerable to sorties. By early February Tatikios' position was untenable so he and his

'The Defeat of Kür-Bugha's' army outside Antioch' in the early 18th-century drawings of the lost 12th-century stained-glass windows of St Denis in Paris. In fact the Crusaders had few horses during this battle.

BELOW **Ruins of the early medieval palace at Raqqa, overlooking the Euphrates in northern Syria, as it appeared in 1971 before being excavated by archaeologists. (Author's photograph)**

troops withdrew to Saint-Symeon, from where they sailed to join the Emperor at Philomelium.

The first attempt to relieve the siege was half-hearted and resulted in the dispersal of a small army led by Duqaq of Damascus and the *amir* of Hama by a similarly small Crusader foraging force under Bohemond of Taranto and Robert of Flanders on 31 December. The troops of Damascus and Hama then apparently continued northward while the Crusader foragers fell back on their outpost at Ariha. Duqaq of Damascus may in fact have been on his way to join a larger relief army assembling at Harenc, between Antioch and Aleppo. The garrison at Harenc had already been raiding Crusader positions around Antioch since late October. Now the forces of Aleppo and Diyarbakr were assembling here and were soon joined by those of Damascus and Hama, under the overall command of Ridwan of Aleppo.

These uncomfortable allies next advanced towards Antioch but were decisively defeated in battle next to the Lake of Antioch on 8 or 9 February 1098. The Crusaders' local Armenian allies occupied Harenc and, despite the fact that the Saljuq garrison set fire to the castle before retreating, the Christians found abundant stores of military equipment and apparently horses there. Tancred's men were supposedly resupplied with this booty, suggesting that one of the smaller Crusader contingents was soon using Islamic arms, armour and horses.

Letters sent home by the Crusaders were by now less optimistic and wrote about real difficulties. The siege of Antioch consisted of an

One of the earliest medieval representations of a crossbow in Europe, dating from the late 11th century. The weapon is being spanned or loaded by a demon. (*In situ* Cathedral of St Sernin, Toulouse; author's photograph)

A late 11th- or 12th-century bridge near the fortified medieval town of Amadiyah in northern Iraq. (Author's photograph)

incomplete blockade, skirmishing in the surrounding countryside and duels between defensive and offensive siege artillery. The treatment of captives may also have become more brutal, Tancred beheading some Turkish prisoners and sending their heads to Bishop Adhémar as a religious tithe. For their part the Turkish garrison hung the heads of Christians convicted of treason on their walls, while efforts to ransom captives seem to have fallen through.

On 4 March 1098 another small fleet arrived at Saint-Symeon. It was described as being English but was not the Anglo-Saxon fleet that already operated under Byzantine command. These newcomers had shown extraordinary determination by sailing during the normally closed winter season. Some stopped at Genoa and Pisa, collecting Italian volunteers on their way, while others may have sailed direct. A few days later the Crusaders decided to build another fort outside the Bridge Gate of Antioch to close an opening through which the garrison could raid communications between the besiegers and the coast.

The eventual fall of Antioch was the result of treachery by one of the garrison's officers. The defenders concentrated along the northern and western walls facing Crusader positions as well as the Gate of St George facing Tancred's Tower in the south. A reliable force would also have been stationed in the Citadel, though communication between the Citadel and the city below would have been difficult because of the cliffs between. At the same time the remaining walls, towers and postern gates of Antioch could not have been ignored. Perhaps Yaghi Siyan made the mistake of leaving these to less reliable troops.

An officer named Firuz al-Zarrad, or Firuz 'the armourer', was seemingly in charge of a tower, postern gate and a stretch of wall on the southeast side of the city. Firuz was a person of some standing and possibly an Armenian convert to Islam. A letter sent by Bohemond to Pope Urban in September 1098, stated, *I, Bohemond, made an agreement with a certain Turk who betrayed the city to me, and with the help of many soldiers of Christ I placed scaling-ladders against the wall shortly before daybreak …*

On 2 June most of the Crusader fighting men assembled south of the city, then marched towards Daphne (Harbiye) as if heading on a foraging raid. However, the Crusader cavalry and infantry divided during the night, before returning to Antioch. The horsemen dismounted just south of the Gate of St George and climbed the steep gorge of the Wadi Zuiba, halting east of the ridge of Mount Silpius. The Crusader infantry probably approached the eastern wall of Antioch along a track directly from Daphne.

A small force of Crusaders under Bohemond of Taranto took control of the tower commanded by Firuz then opened a postern gate to allow the rest of their unit to penetrate the defences before dawn on 3 June. An attack by a larger force under Godfrey of Bouillon on the Citadel was repulsed. By daybreak Bohemond's men had seized 'ten towers' and raised a banner on the southern peak of Mount Silpius. The remaining Christian population of Antioch attacked the Saljuq garrison in the city, which indicates that Yaghi Siyan had only expelled their leaders and those regarded as unreliable at the start of the siege. Yaghi Siyan apparently believed that the Citadel had fallen and immediately fled the city but was killed by Armenian irregulars north of Idlib. Much of the garrison fled up the mountainside to the Citadel as the Crusaders broke in, many being killed while climbing the cliffs. Having failed to take the Citadel, the Crusaders on Mount Silpius entered the city, almost certainly through the Iron Gate to the north.

All that remains of the 12th-century Saljuq palace in Mosul is a reception hall or throne room overlooking the river Tigris. (Author's photograph)

The most personal account of the taking of Antioch comes from a letter, written in the name of the city of Lucca, to spread an account of an eyewitness. This individual, Bruno of Lucca, had reported: *There were four kinsmen, noble men of Antioch, and on the second day of June they promised to surrender the city to Bohemond, Robert Curthose, and Robert Count of Flanders. But with the common consent of all our princes, they conducted the whole army to the wall of the city at nightfall, without the knowledge of the Turks. In the morning, when the citizens of Antioch opened the gates expecting to receive the three named princes alone … all our men suddenly charged in together. There was a great din. Our men occupied all the strong points, except the highest citadel. As to the Turks, some they killed, some they hurled to destruction over the precipice.*

All sources emphasise the slaughter in Antioch, as Bohemond of Taranto himself recorded: 'We kept their wives, children and servants, together with their gold, silver and all their possessions.'

The 'Abbasid Caliph in Baghdad tried to generate support and assistance for the defenders of Antioch during the siege, and had urged the Great Saljuq Sultan Berk Yaruq to send reinforcements. However, the Sultan's own forces were busy in eastern Iran, so he reportedly ordered Kür-Bugha, governor of Mosul, to save Antioch. In fact relations between Kür-Bugha and Berk Yaruq were difficult and the ruler of Mosul may have acted on his own initiative, assembling his forces around Mosul and heading west.

Eventually the 'armies of Syria, its Turks and Arabs', with the exception of Ridwan of Aleppo, joined Kür-Bugha near Aleppo. The reasons for Ridwan's absence were varied and, being in bitter rivalry with Duqaq of Damascus, he may not have felt safe joining a force where Duqaq played a senior role. Nevertheless, Ridwan did allow the allies to gather within his own territory.

The Islamic forces assembled at Marj Dabiq near Qinnisrin, which had long been a traditional mustering area for armies because it contained abundant pastures for their horses. But before arriving, Kür-Bugha attempted to retake Edessa from Count Baldwin. This unsuccessful siege lasted three weeks, during which time the Crusaders took Antioch. However, Kür-Bugha did arrive with an impressive army, having been joined by some other Saljuq *amirs* along the way. At Marj Dabiq he was also joined by contingents from Hims, Damascus and Diyarbakr. The allied army probably reached the river Orontes at the 'Iron Bridge' on 5 June, appearing before Crusader-held Antioch four days later.

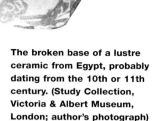

Some historians estimate that the Crusaders were now down to 100–200 properly mounted knights; the rest being obliged to fight on foot alongside the infantry. This might be an exaggeration, but the greater proportion of the army that challenged Kür-Bugha was on foot. This limited, though it certainly did not destroy, the effectiveness of the knights.

According to the *Gesta Francorum*, some captured Crusader weapons were shown to Kür-Bugha before the battle, including 'a very poor sword all covered with rust, a thoroughly bad wooden bow [not of composite construction] and a spear which was quite useless'. Furthermore the alliance between Byzantines, Crusaders and Armenians had largely evaporated after the taking of Antioch, so the Crusader host was now on its own.

The broken base of a lustre ceramic from Egypt, probably dating from the 10th or 11th century. (Study Collection, Victoria & Albert Museum, London; author's photograph)

'The Betrayal' in an Armenian *Gospel* made in AD1057. (Ms. 362.G, Patriarchal Library, Etchmiadzin)

The confrontation that followed was remarkable because the Crusaders won despite being in an apparently hopeless situation. Ibn al-Athir even wrote that some Crusader leaders tried to make a deal with Kür-Bugha before the battle in return for being allowed to go home. Much of the Crusader host was, however, now in a state of religious excitement that had been increased, though not caused, by the finding of the so-called 'Holy Lance' on 14 June. The significance of this object was certainly emphasised in later accounts of the victory. Divisions between rich and poor were breaking down in this extraordinary atmosphere and the Crusader host was becoming a religiously motivated horde.

More prosaically, the unfortunate Kür-Bugha was abandoned by many of his allies for reasons of short-sighted Saljuq internal rivalry. There were tensions between Turcoman and Arab nomad troops within his army as well as mistrust between Turks and Arabic-speaking urban Muslims. Of course Kür-Bugha tried to impose discipline on his fragmented forces and probably believed that by defeating the invaders he could unite the other Saljuq governors behind him.

On 5 June Kür-Bugha's army established camp near the Kara Su stream north of Antioch, perhaps around a spring or well that still exists. By 7 June his troops had forced Crusader outposts back inside the city. Next day Kür-Bugha led a substantial force up into the hills to contact the Saljuq garrison still holding the Citadel. A flanking attack by Crusader forces failed to prevent this and for the next few days Saljuq troops tried to retake the city from the Citadel. Since they could not advance directly down the precipice they tried to work their way along the fortifications, but the Crusaders constructed a rough stone wall, almost certainly from inside the fortifications south of the Citadel to the edge of the cliff. This stopped the Turks from outflanking the Crusaders' hold on the wall. On 14 June Kür-Bugha abandoned this attempt and returned to lower ground where his troops completed their investment of the city. Like the Crusaders before them, they concentrated on the northern and western walls while sending one contingent to block the Gate of St George.

The defeat of Kür-Bugha

Bohemond of Taranto was supervising commander when the Crusaders decided to challenge Kür-Bugha in the open. It was a remarkable decision dictated as much by the Crusaders' state of mind as their low supplies. Bohemond expected a very hard fight and held back much of the Crusaders' strength in reserve. Meanwhile Raymond of Toulouse and part of the Provençal contingent remained on Mount Silpius to ensure that the Citadel garrison did not take part in the battle.

Early on 28 June 1098 most of the Crusader host emerged from the Bridge Gate, headed by Godfrey of Bouillon and the other northern

The courtyard of the *Juma'a* or Congregational Mosque at Ma'arat al-Nu'man in Syria. Most of what is seen here dates from before the First Crusade. (Author's photograph)

OPPOSITE **The island of Arwad, three kilometres from the Syrian coast facing the city of Tartus.** (Author's photograph)

French contingents. They were attacked by Turkish units facing this gate and the fact that Hugh of Vermandois could counter-attack suggests he had many of the Crusaders' remaining cavalry under his command. Kür-Bugha now called off the Turkish attack, a decision unlikely to have been a result of Hugh of Vermandois' counter-stroke. Some sources indicate that he wanted to get all the Crusaders outside Antioch so that he could then destroy them entirely. This would have avoided a prolonged siege with the tensions that could impose on his fragile coalition, but although it was a tactically astute decision it was politically misguided.

According to Ibn al-Athir, writing a century later, Janah al-Dawla of Hims and Sökmen Ibn Artuk, who held Diyarbakr, Suruç and Jerusalem, had been placed 'in ambush'. It is possible that instead of simply calling off the initial attack, Kür-Bugha planned a traditional feigned retreat to lure the Crusader host into this ambush. Perhaps Janah and Sökmen were positioned outside the Dog and St Paul's gates. Ibn al-Athir indicates that other un-named 'rebel *amirs*' used this withdrawal as an opportunity to abandon the field, but suggests that the rulers of Hims and Jerusalem were amongst the last to flee. Ibn al-Athir went on to say that, 'The only Muslims to stand firm were a detachment … from the Holy Land [Palestine] who fought to acquire merit in God's eyes and to seek martyrdom.' Such religiously motivated volunteers would have been almost entirely on foot and so had little chance of escape.

ABOVE **'A Soldier at the Betrayal' on the early 12th-century bronze *Font de Notre Dames du Fonts*. (*In situ* Church of St Barthélemy, Liège)**

Bohemond did not send his whole force forward as the enemy withdrew. Since most of the Crusaders were on foot it would have been difficult to pursue the Turks anyway. The small Saljuq unit watching the Gate of St George now moved around to support those outside the Bridge Gate. They were driven back by Renard of Toul's contingent, which was part of the reserve. Saljuq cavalry probably moved across the Crusader front around this time to stop a flanking move by Bishop Adhémar or as part of the plot to abandon Kür-Bugha. Adhémar's southern French contingent was clearly slowed down by piecemeal attacks. This left much of the Islamic infantry to face the main Crusader force that now advanced.

It may have been at this stage that some religiously inflamed Crusaders saw what they interpreted as celestial warriors on the neighbouring hills, coming to support Christ's soldiers. Such stories would obviously have been emphasised later, to explain the enemy's otherwise unaccountable flight. The exact course of events is impossible to ascertain, yet it seems that the withdrawing Saljuq infantry contingents crossed the Wadi al-Qifaysiya and made a stand on a low hill. They were driven off and it was probably during an increasingly disorganised retreat that some tried to set fire to the dry grass to slow the Crusader pursuit.

Bishop Adhémar's contingent presumably reached the Wadi al-Qifaysiya, threatening the flank of Kür-Bugha's contingent, which was now advancing. What happened next is even less clear. Either Kür-Bugha's followers retreated in disorder when they saw so much of the allied army abandoning the field or some of them were actually involved in the plot to betray Kür-Bugha. Both seem unlikely as Kür-Bugha's contingent probably consisted of his own elite 'askar of ghulams or mamluks, plus Turcoman levies and militia infantry who would have had little hope of escape if abandoned by their cavalry. Whatever really happened, Kür-Bugha withdrew hastily after setting fire to his camp. Seeing the collapse of the allied army, the garrison in the Citadel of Antioch surrendered, perhaps trapped by Raymond of Toulouse.

When the Crusaders overran Kür-Bugha's camp they reportedly massacred those who remained. Bohemond himself sent Kür-Bugha's perhaps charred tent home as a trophy. On the other hand the *Gesta Francorum* refers to many elite *ghulam* troops being captured: 'The agulani numbered three thousand. They feared neither spears nor arrows nor any other weapon for they and their horses are covered all over with plates of iron [lamellar armour for man and horse].' Some converted to Christianity and probably reappeared later in the story of the First Crusade, as did certain Jews who were captured either in Antioch or Kür-Bugha's camp.

ABOVE: **Foot soldiers armed with spears and large round shields, on Norman late 11th- or early 12th-century carved capital. (***In situ*** parish church, Rucquerville; author's photograph)**

THE MARCH ON JERUSALEM

The deaths of a large number of Muslim foot soldiers from the Holy Land outside Antioch would have had an impact in Jerusalem, both militarily and politically. Saljuq Turkish rule was not popular in Palestine, and Sökmen Ibn Artuk may well have been blamed for deserting his infantry. The Fatimid government decided to take advantage of Saljuq difficulties and so the Grand Vizier al-Afdal led his own *'askar* to seize Jerusalem.

According to Ibn al-Qalanisi, al-Afdal made camp and demanded that Sökmen Ibn Artuk, 'surrender Jerusalem to him without warfare or shedding of blood'. When the Turks refused he attacked with 'many mangonels' that breached the wall, whereupon Sökmen surrendered. Ibn al-Athir stated that the fighting went on for more than six weeks and the fact that al-Afdal's mangonels could breach stone fortifications is part of growing evidence that some form of counterweight trebuchet was known earlier than is generally believed. Al-Maqrizi, in his account

THE BATTLE OUTSIDE ANTIOCH (pages 62–63)

When the Crusader army emerged from Antioch under the overall command of Bohemond of Taranto, the Saljuq commander Kür-Bugha ordered his men not to attack them in force. Instead they were to wait until all the enemy were outside the shelter of Antioch's walls. Kür-Bugha may have been hoping to draw the Crusader force into a classic ambush, using feigned retreat tactics, and would almost certainly have tried to separate the Crusaders' cavalry from their infantry. He then seems to have been betrayed by several subordinate commanders who feared that victory would make Kür-Bugha too powerful. In fact the Crusader army now contained so few horses that there were virtually no cavalry units to detach from the foot soldiers who, by this time, formed the vast majority of the Christian horde (1). Troops from southern France (2) seem to have been in a better state than most others, probably because they formed part of the well-organised army of Raymond of Toulouse. Raymond was also rich and seems to have been able to obtain some horses locally (3). Since so much horse-harness had been abandoned during the Crusaders' appalling trek across the Anatolian mountains, many would now have been using Middle Eastern saddles and bridles. Some northern French (4), Lotharingians (5) and Italo-Normans (6) also had horses, but a great many knights now fought on foot (7), alongside archers (8) and others who had walked all the way from Western Europe. At the same time there is strong evidence that captured Middle Eastern weaponry, such as the typical Islamic mace (9), was being used. Under normal circumstances the outnumbered and half starved Christians should have lost. This was not, however, a normal battle. A large part of the Islamic army abandoned the field without a fight while most of the Crusaders seemed to have been in a state of almost hysterical religious intoxication (10). After victory was won, many Crusaders reported seeing white angelic horsemen in the clouds above the battle (11), which would, from their fanatical point of view, have accounted for the seemingly 'miraculous' panic that gripped their Muslim foes.

(Christa Hook)

The citadel of Shayzar, overlooking the river Orontes in central Syria. (Author's photograph)

of these events, wrote that al-Afdal, 'recovered the Holy City from the Armenians', perhaps indicating that the Saljuq garrison included Christian Armenians.

The Saljuq commanders were well treated and allowed to go free, travelling through Damascus and across the Euphrates to Suruç, another Artukid possession. Al-Afdal took his army back to Egypt, but left Iftikhar al-Dawla as the Fatimid governor in Jerusalem with a small garrison of Sudanese infantry plus an elite of around 400 Arab cavalry. Iftikhar was also instructed to repair the damaged fortifications. Tyre (Sur) had already been retaken from a disloyal governor in 1097 and the defences of Sidon (Saida) were restored in 1098. It is also interesting to note that the Fatimid garrison of Acre in 1098 probably included Armenian troops and that one of their officers was Bahram al-Armani, an Armenian nobleman from Turbessel (Tal Bashir) who later became the Fatimid Caliph's Christian Grand Vizier.

Apparently the Fatimids still regarded the Saljuqs as a greater threat than the Crusaders. In the event the Fatimid-ruled coastal cities were seemingly instructed to make their own arrangements when the Crusaders crossed the Fatimid frontier at the Dog River (Nahr al-Kalb), though the garrison of Jerusalem may have been strengthened and food stocks were assembled inside the city. Only after the Crusaders had attacked did Al-Afdal promise to bring a relief army by the end of July.

The Crusader host remained around Antioch until 11 December 1098. They could not leave it to be retaken by the Saljuqs and several leaders would have preferred the Byzantine authorities to take over. The rank-and-file were less keen to hand the city over to the Byzantines and when Alexios withdrew in western Anatolia the Crusaders tried to sort the Antioch problem out for themselves. Meanwhile their cavalry attempted to obtain remounts from local stocks. Reinforcements arrived by sea in small numbers, 1,500 reportedly landing at Saint-Symeon in August, though most then died of disease.

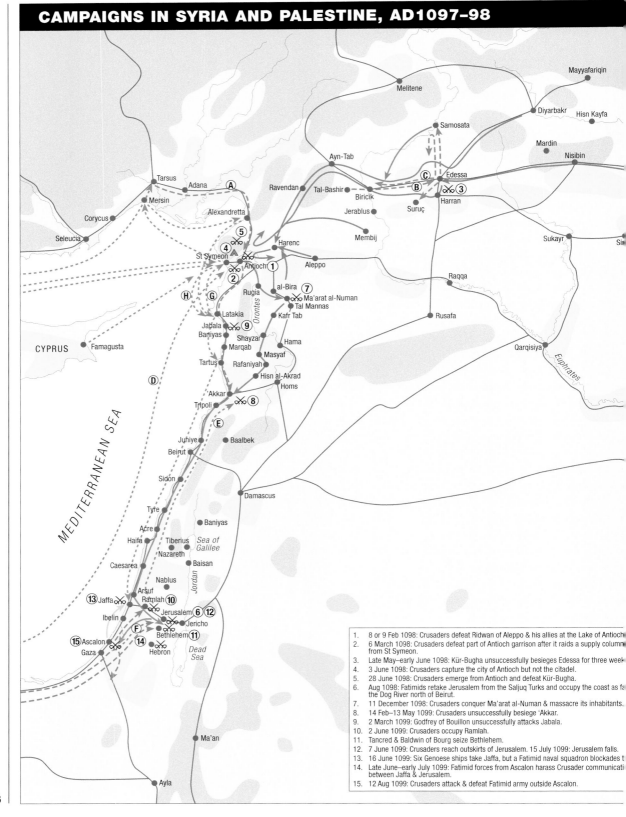

1. 8 or 9 Feb 1098: Crusaders defeat Ridwan of Aleppo & his allies at the Lake of Antioch
2. 6 March 1098: Crusaders defeat part of Antioch garrison after it raids a supply column from St Symeon.
3. Late May–early June 1098: Kür-Bugha unsuccessfully besieges Edessa for three week
4. 3 June 1098: Crusaders capture the city of Antioch but not the citadel.
5. 28 June 1098: Crusaders emerge from Antioch and defeat Kür-Bugha.
6. Aug 1098: Fatimids retake Jerusalem from the Saljuq Turks and occupy the coast as fa the Dog River north of Beirut.
7. 11 December 1098: Crusaders conquer Ma'arat al-Numan & massacre its inhabitants.
8. 14 Feb–13 May 1099: Crusaders unsuccessfully besiege 'Akkar.
9. 2 March 1099: Godfrey of Bouillon unsuccessfully attacks Jabala.
10. 2 June 1099: Crusaders occupy Ramlah.
11. Tancred & Baldwin of Bourg seize Bethlehem.
12. 7 June 1099: Crusaders reach outskirts of Jerusalem. 15 July 1099: Jerusalem falls.
13. 16 June 1099: Six Genoese ships take Jaffa, but a Fatimid naval squadron blockades t
14. Late June–early July 1099: Fatimid forces from Ascalon harass Crusader communicati between Jaffa & Jerusalem.
15. 12 Aug 1099: Crusaders attack & defeat Fatimid army outside Ascalon.

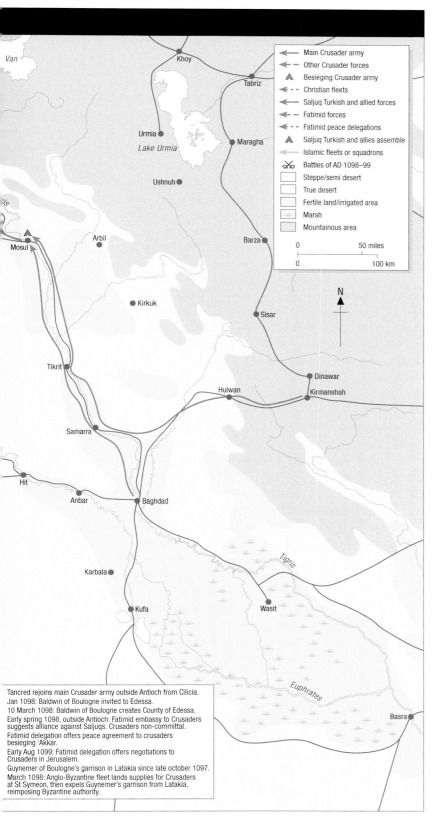

Map legend:

- Main Crusader army
- Other Crusader forces
- Besieging Crusader army
- Christian fleets
- Saljuq Turkish and allied forces
- Fatimid forces
- Fatimid peace delegations
- Saljuq Turkish and allies assemble
- Islamic fleets or squadrons
- Battles of AD 1098–99
- Steppe/semi desert
- True desert
- Fertile land/irrigated area
- Marsh
- Mountainous area

0   50 miles
0   100 km

N

Tancred rejoins main Crusader army outside Antioch from Cilicia.
Jan 1098: Baldwin of Boulogne invited to Edessa.
10 March 1098: Baldwin of Boulogne creates County of Edessa.
Early spring 1098, outside Antioch: Fatimid embassy to Crusaders suggests alliance against Saljuqs. Crusaders non-committal.
Fatimid delegation offers peace agreement to crusaders besieging 'Akkar.
Early Aug 1099: Fatimid delegation offers negotiations to Crusaders in Jerusalem.
Guynemer of Boulogne's garrison in Latakia since late october 1097.
March 1098: Anglo-Byzantine fleet lands supplies for Crusaders at St Symeon, then expels Guynemer's garrison from Latakia, reimposing Byzantine authority.

Map labels: Van, Khoy, Tabriz, Urmia, Lake Urmia, Maragha, Ushnuh, Arbil, Mosul, Barza, Sisar, Kirkuk, Tikrit, Dinawar, Hulwan, Kirmanshah, Samarra, Hit, Anbar, Baghdad, Karbala, Kufa, Wasit, Tigris, Euphrates, Basra

Huntsman fighting a lion and using his cloak as a shield on an 11th- or 12th-century carved ivory panel, probably from Egypt. (Museo Nazionale del Bargello, Florence; author's photograph)

Negotiations with Fatimid envoys showed there was no threat from that direction, or from the fragmented Saljuqs. Crusader messengers supposedly assured Duqaq of Damascus that they did not intend to attack, though he clearly felt threatened from both north and south. The Islamic governor of A'zaz who had rebelled against Ridwan of Aleppo now accepted Godfrey of Bouillon as his overlord in return for military support.

Many ordinary Crusaders were, however, growing restless. When a castle near Ma'arat al-Nu'man was seized in July, those captured were offered conversion or death. Elsewhere Christian priests baptised dying Muslims after battle, whether they wished it or not. When Raymond of Toulouse captured al-Bara in September the population was slaughtered. Meanwhile it took a long time to decide who would become lord of Antioch. The Byzantines expected Bohemond of Taranto to take over and as early as 14 July 1098 Bohemond was issuing commercial privileges to the Genoese. Eventually Bohemond's followers expelled those of his rival, Raymond of Toulouse, by force.

The biggest military operation during this period was the capture of Ma'arat al-Nu'man on 11 December 1098, which resulted in some of the most horrifying episodes in the history of the First Crusade. According to Ibn al-Athir some of the city's defenders, probably the professional garrison, abandoned the outer wall and tried to use one of the town's largest buildings as a fortress. This led other defenders, probably the local militia, to abandon the wall and fall back to defend their own homes. At this point the Crusaders entered the city and massacred its population. Many Crusaders were now desperate for food and a handful turned to cannibalism. This was when the *Tafurs* appeared as a coherent group of desperate fanatics under their own leaders. The latter were probably knights who had lost the equipment that gave them status. By this time the Crusade's senior leadership had similarly used up almost all their resources. An eclipse of the sun in December 1098 contributed to the general hysteria.

Several Arabic chroniclers recorded the events at Ma'arat al-Nu'man with obvious horror, including Ibn al-'Adim: 'They killed a great number under torture. They extorted people's treasure. They prevented people from getting water, and then sold it to them. Most of the people died of thirst.' A surviving letter from a merchant described the devastation: 'My friend, I am from a city which God has condemned to be destroyed. They have killed all its inhabitants, putting old men and children to the sword.' Another anonymous poet wrote; 'I do not know if it is a grazing ground for wild beast or is my home, my native town.'

A month later Raymond of Toulouse headed south at the head of thousands of people, including a large number of the Crusader 'poor'. The rulers of Shayzar and Hims, with military forces numbering hundreds rather than thousands, could not hope to resist such hordes and gave them free passage and even supplies. On 14 February Raymond besieged the fortified town of 'Akkar, whose garrison was loyal to the *amir* of Tripoli. Three days later Raymond Pilet, a Provençal knight seized the coastal city of Tartus, whereupon the nearby castle of Marqab also surrendered. Control of Tartus gave the Crusaders another port but further south Christian ships would be venturing into Fatimid waters.

Many Crusader rank-and-file now suspected their leaders of mere land grabbing. There is strong evidence that Raymond of Toulouse did want to carve out a state for himself based upon Tripoli, but Raymond probably also felt he had to take 'Akkar because his forces were small, he was deep in Islamic territory, a long way from Antioch and was getting close to the Fatimid frontier. In February a great red aurora was seen in the sky, again heightening religious fervour, and in May the Anglo-Saxon crews of the remaining nine or ten Byzantine ships burned their vessels and joined the march south. Troops were also leaving the

The 'Four Nourias' or medieval waterwheels powered by the river Orontes, on the northern outskirts of the Syrian city of Hama. (Author's photograph)

'Soldiers at the Crucifixion', in a Byzantine wall painting made in the 10th century. (*In situ* Toprak Kilise no.7, Göreme; author's photograph)

contingents of Godfrey of Bouillon, Robert of Flanders and Bohemond of Taranto in Antioch, preferring to join Raymond's thrust south. In February the three commanders bowed to popular pressure and led their armies to Latakia, though Bohemond left them there and returned to undisputed control of Antioch.

Godfrey and Robert besieged Jabala but raised this in return for tribute on hearing that Raymond of Toulouse feared an attack outside 'Akkar. Jabala, like Tartus, probably formed part of the coastal *amirate* of the Banu 'Ammar, a Shi'a Arab dynasty that ruled Tripoli. Even after these two contingents joined Raymond, 'Akkar refused to fall. Another Fatimid embassy now arrived in the Crusader camp.

It now seems that discussions between this Fatimid embassy and the Crusader leadership involved the possibility of joint operations against the Saljuqs and the restoration of various cities to the Fatimid Caliphate in return for the Christians having Jerusalem. At the time the Fatimid government seems to have been torn between an alliance with the Crusaders against the Turks, and with the Turks against the Crusaders. One Crusader source even suggests that some local Saljuq leaders offered to pay tribute to the Fatimids in return for an alliance and even to 'worship Alim' or 'Ali, in other words to become Shi'a rather than Sunni Muslims. In the end the religious fanaticism that was driving the Crusader rank-and-file made an accommodation with the Fatimids impossible. So, on 16 March 1099, the investment of 'Akkar was raised and the Crusader host resumed its trek southward.

This time they clung to the narrow coastal plain that placed the towering mountains of Lebanon between the invaders and the powerful *amirate* of Damascus. The ruler of Tripoli supposedly agreed that, if the Crusaders defeated the Fatimids, he would 'convert to Christianity' and hold his lands under Crusader suzerainty. Though the idea of conversion

OPPOSITE **'David returning with the head of Goliath' in a Byzantine *Psalter* made around AD1088. The young warrior is on horseback, as was occasionally the case in Eastern Christian art. (Codex 761, f. 13v, Vatopedi Monastery Library, Mount Athos)**

The Lebanese coast just outside Beirut. Here there is no coastal plain and the north–south road runs right along the shore. (Author's photograph)

should not be taken seriously, part of an otherwise lost chronicle stated that an envoy from the *amir* of Tripoli accompanied Raymond of Toulouse to smooth Crusader relations with cities further south.

After crossed the Dog river north of Beirut the Crusaders entered Fatimid territory, where several local governors supplied the intruders with money, food and guides in return for no damage to the surrounding agricultural area. But the Fatimid governor of Sidon refused to cooperate and his garrison attacked the Crusader host when it looted local villages. The towns further south generally followed the example of Beirut and by the time the Crusaders reached Acre they seem to have learned a lot about local religious and political rivalries. However, the fact that Bahram al-Armani, a Christian Armenian officer in Fatimid service (see p.65), felt it necessary to 'escape the Franks' at Acre suggests tensions within these coastal garrisons.

Reaching Arsuf in early June, the Crusaders turned inland. A tiny Fatimid garrison at Jaffa attempted to raze their fortifications before retreating to Ascalon, though an anonymous Syriac chronicle stated that the invaders did besiege Jaffa for a few days. Most of the inland towns and villages of Palestine were evacuated by their Muslim inhabitants before the Crusaders arrived. On the other hand some local leaders remained. For example, a former 'Saracen ruler' from Ramlah, the traditional capital of Islamic Palestine, supposedly converted to Christianity and later accompanied the Crusader army against the Fatimids outside Ascalon. This man may have been the local *rai's* or headman and was as likely to have been a Christian as a Muslim. On the night of 6/7 June, Tancred and Baldwin of Bourg seized Bethlehem and the main Crusader army arrived outside Jerusalem itself on the 7th.

By violating the Fatimid frontier the Crusaders were challenging a significant naval power. The Fatimid fleet was powerful with over 70 warships. The bulk of the fleet was normally based at naval bases at Cairo, Alexandria, Damietta and Tinnis in Egypt, with other smaller squadrons based in Ascalon and Acre, and occasionally at Tyre and Beirut, on the Palestine/Lebanon coast. Consequently the Christian squadrons did not follow the Crusader host but only sailed as far as Tartus. South of Tripoli any Crusader ships would also be unable to come ashore to replenish their water supplies without the danger of being attacked by local garrisons. In fact, when the army marched south, the Crusader and Byzantine ships seem to have withdrawn to Crusader-held Tartus and Byzantine-held Latakia. Between these the third port of Jabala was still in Islamic hands and would remain so until 1109. The Pisan fleet that clashed with the Byzantines on its voyage east, reached Syria in late summer 1099 and joined Bohemond, now the Prince of Antioch, in unsuccessfully attacking Byzantine Latakia.

The Saljuq rulers of northern Syria had also returned to their traditional quarrelling. Ridwan of Aleppo felt particularly vulnerable, with Bohemond of Antioch as one neighbour and Janah al-Dawla of Hims as another. The Artuqid governor of Diyarbakr summoned Sökmen Ibn Artuk, late governor of Jerusalem, to help him against Kür-Bugha, who may have been trying to re-establish a dominant position following his defeat outside Antioch. In the event Sökmen Ibn Artuk was driven off. It seemed, in fact, to be business as usual.

THE SIEGE OF JERUSALEM

Jerusalem in 1099 was a thriving city, though it was neither as large nor as important as it had been in early Islamic times. After a period of decline, it had revived in the 10th century under Fatimid rule. The city's Jewish population had also expanded, especially the Karaite or non-orthodox community, which was similar in size to the Rabbinical or orthodox community. The Jewish population slumped during Saljuq rule and those that remained clearly welcomed the Fatimids' return in 1098. A year later the Crusader conquest destroyed the community entirely.

A major earthquake had ruined much of Jerusalem in 1033, destroying many of its fortifications. The Fatimid government immediately rebuilt them, often using masonry from ruined churches, but also reduced the area enclosed by these defences. As a result the old Jewish quarter south of the Temple Mount was now outside the new fortifications so the Jews were allocated a new area in the northeastern corner of Jerusalem. This was still called the Jewish Quarter under Crusader rule, though it was no longer Jewish. The Christians were allocated the northwestern corner of Jerusalem while Muslims lived in the southern part of the city.

Much of southeastern Jerusalem consisted of the Temple Mount or Haram al-Sharif, which was a religious rather than domestic or commercial area. Several Christian monasteries were built near the Church of the Holy Sepulchre under Fatimid rule but the following brief period of Saljuq occupation was a time of disruption, destruction and persecution, not only of Christians and Jews but also of Shi'a Muslims.

As the Crusader host approached, the governor in Jerusalem, Iftikhar al-Dawla, took precautionary measures, though he may not have been certain the intruders would attack. He ordered that wells outside the city be polluted to deny an enemy drinking water and had animal herds driven out of range so that they could not be seized as food. Labourers prepared timber beams ready for use in defensive machines while other timber in the area was hidden, sometimes in caves. Most of the Christian population of Jerusalem was also temporarily expelled from Jerusalem though the Jews remained to help in its defence.

This expulsion of Christians makes it unlikely that the Fatimid garrison included Armenian soldiers. Many senior Christian figures were already absent, having fled the Saljuqs and not yet returned. Yet some Christians clearly remained, including Gerard (later called 'The Blessed'), who was the guardian of the Amalfitan hospices within Jerusalem. He remained throughout the siege and was still there when the Crusaders took over. Only now did the Fatimid Grand Vizier al-Afdal apparently realise that the Crusader threat was real, so he began

Easter celebrations in the early medieval Church of the Nativity in Bethlehem.

assembling an army to cross the Sinai Desert to Ascalon, from where he hoped to raise the siege of Jerusalem.

As the Crusaders assembled outside Jerusalem, they probably numbered a fighting strength of 12,000, including 1,200–1,300 knights, plus a far greater number of male and female non-combatants. Though the Crusader host was far larger than the defending garrison and militia, they could not surround the entire city without spreading their fighting men too thinly. So the Crusaders divisions formed up around the northwestern corner of Jerusalem, with Raymond of Toulouse on the right, Godfrey and Tancred in the centre, Robert of Normandy and Robert of Flanders on the left.

Their first attack on 13 June was pressed with fanatical enthusiasm, perhaps believing that the city would fall of its own accord. They were, however, so short of timber that they could construct only one assault ladder, which was placed between the divisions of Tancred and the two Roberts. During this first assault Iftikhar al-Dawla probably had his headquarters where the so-called Quadrilateral Tower would later be built, while the Fatimid garrison and Jerusalem militia manned the wall facing the invader divisions. Iftikhar's Arab reserve would probably have been held back at this stage.

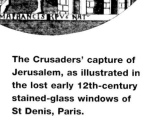

The Crusaders' capture of Jerusalem, as illustrated in the lost early 12th-century stained-glass windows of St Denis, Paris.

It was soon clear that the defenders' military engines were effective and numerous. These were normally mounted on towers and were made of better materials than those available to the Crusaders. According to William of Tyre: 'This was comparatively easy, for the people of Jerusalem had at their command many more skilled workmen and building tools, as well as larger supplies of iron, copper, ropes and so on than had our people.' A recently translated account states that one machine was on the gate besieged by the Count of Toulouse, probably meaning the Jaffa Gate or the neighbouring Citadel. It was capable of hurling incendiary missiles against the Provençal camp and the resulting fires put great strain on the Crusaders' inadequate water supplies. Women helped douse the flames and took drinking water to the soldiers while old or unfit men helped construct a machine to counter the Fatimid engine. It appears to have been a three-pronged iron hook suspended by an iron chain, probably attached to a long beam on a timber frame, perhaps being intended to snare or topple the Fatimid weapon. Their iron hook was, however, thrown off by one of the defenders, who, though unarmoured, placed himself in full view of the Crusaders' archers and crossbowmen.

After their first assault was defeated the Crusaders settled down to a proper siege, not attempting another major attack for a month. During the intervening period they were reinforced by latecomers or stragglers, and some western soldiers who had served in this area for years. One was Hugh Bunel who had been in the Middle East for 20 years, after being exiled from France for murder. What the besiegers needed most, however, were materials to construct siege machines.

On 17 June six Christian galleys arrived at Jaffa from Tartus. Two were certainly Genoese, being commanded by Guglielmo and Primo Embriaco, and the others were probably Genoese. They had not only defied Fatimid patrols but had sailed far beyond the range of their water

The Old City of Jerusalem seen from the southwest before the Israeli occupation of 1967.

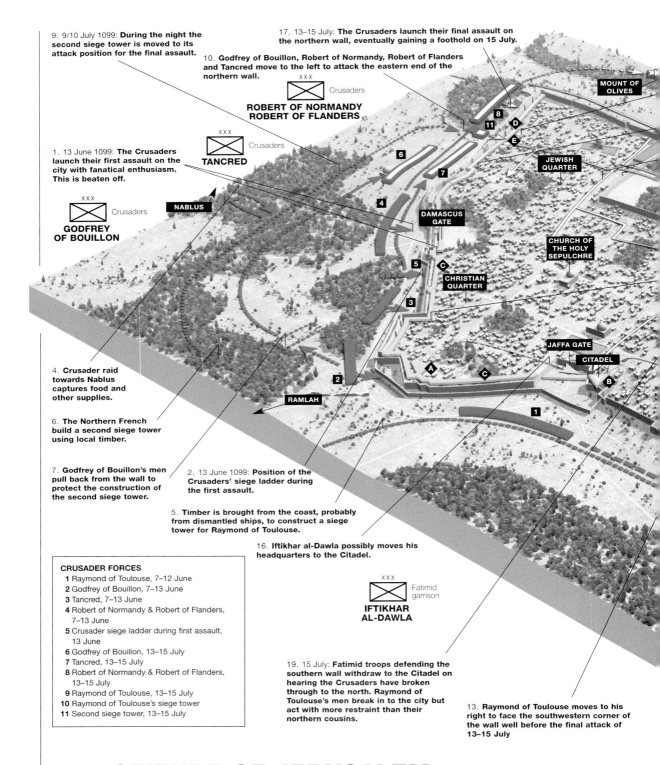

9. **9/10 July 1099:** During the night the second siege tower is moved to its attack position for the final assault.

17. **13–15 July:** The Crusaders launch their final assault on the northern wall, eventually gaining a foothold on 15 July.

10. **Godfrey of Bouillon, Robert of Normandy, Robert of Flanders and Tancred move to the left to attack the eastern end of the northern wall.**

XXX
ROBERT OF NORMANDY
ROBERT OF FLANDERS
Crusaders

XXX
TANCRED
Crusaders

1. **13 June 1099:** The Crusaders launch their first assault on the city with fanatical enthusiasm. This is beaten off.

XXX
GODFREY
OF BOUILLON
Crusaders

NABLUS

MOUNT OF OLIVES

8

11

D

E

6

7

JEWISH QUARTER

4

DAMASCUS GATE

CHURCH OF THE HOLY SEPULCHRE

5

C

CHRISTIAN QUARTER

3

JAFFA GATE

CITADEL

A

C

B

2

1

RAMLAH

4. **Crusader raid towards Nablus captures food and other supplies.**

6. **The Northern French build a second siege tower using local timber.**

7. **Godfrey of Bouillon's men pull back from the wall to protect the construction of the second siege tower.**

2. **13 June 1099:** Position of the Crusaders' siege ladder during the first assault.

5. **Timber is brought from the coast, probably from dismantled ships, to construct a siege tower for Raymond of Toulouse.**

16. **Iftikhar al-Dawla possibly moves his headquarters to the Citadel.**

XXX
IFTIKHAR
AL-DAWLA
Fatimid garrison

CRUSADER FORCES
1 Raymond of Toulouse, 7–12 June
2 Godfrey of Bouillon, 7–13 June
3 Tancred, 7–13 June
4 Robert of Normandy & Robert of Flanders, 7–13 June
5 Crusader siege ladder during first assault, 13 June
6 Godfrey of Bouillon, 13–15 July
7 Tancred, 13–15 July
8 Robert of Normandy & Robert of Flanders, 13–15 July
9 Raymond of Toulouse, 13–15 July
10 Raymond of Toulouse's siege tower
11 Second siege tower, 13–15 July

19. **15 July:** Fatimid troops defending the southern wall withdraw to the Citadel on hearing the Crusaders have broken through to the north. Raymond of Toulouse's men break in to the city but act with more restraint than their northern cousins.

13. **Raymond of Toulouse moves to his right to face the southwestern corner of the wall well before the final attack of 13–15 July**

THE SEIZURE OF JERUSALEM

June–July 1099, viewed from the southwest showing the initial, unsuccessful Crusader assault on the city and the preparations for the final successful assault, which culminates in a horrific massacre of the Muslim and Jewish populations of the city.

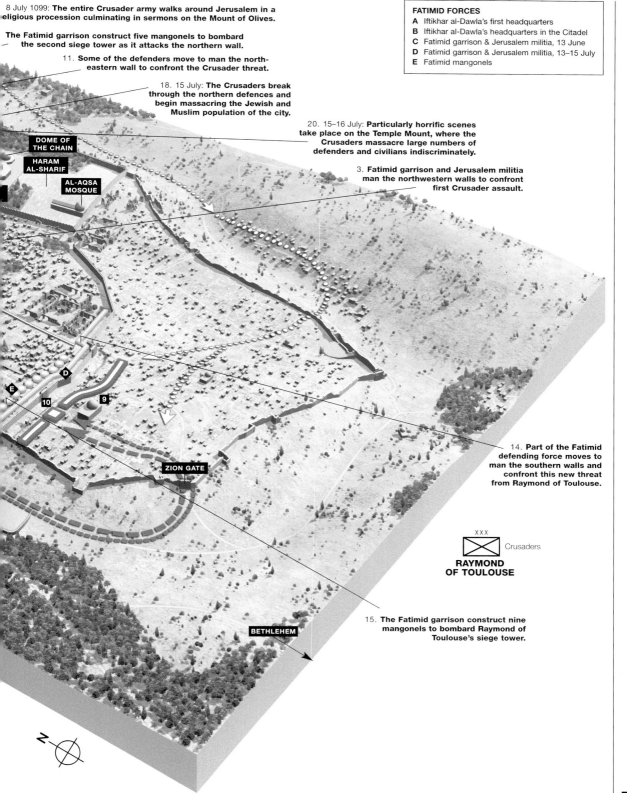

8 July 1099: **The entire Crusader army walks around Jerusalem in a religious procession culminating in sermons on the Mount of Olives.**

The Fatimid garrison construct five mangonels to bombard the second siege tower as it attacks the northern wall.

11. **Some of the defenders move to man the north-eastern wall to confront the Crusader threat.**

18. 15 July: **The Crusaders break through the northern defences and begin massacring the Jewish and Muslim population of the city.**

20. 15–16 July: **Particularly horrific scenes take place on the Temple Mount, where the Crusaders massacre large numbers of defenders and civilians indiscriminately.**

3. **Fatimid garrison and Jerusalem militia man the northwestern walls to confront first Crusader assault.**

FATIMID FORCES
A Iftikhar al-Dawla's first headquarters
B Iftikhar al-Dawla's headquarters in the Citadel
C Fatimid garrison & Jerusalem militia, 13 June
D Fatimid garrison & Jerusalem militia, 13–15 July
E Fatimid mangonels

DOME OF THE CHAIN

HARAM AL-SHARIF

AL-AQSA MOSQUE

D

E

10

9

ZION GATE

14. **Part of the Fatimid defending force moves to man the southern walls and confront this new threat from Raymond of Toulouse.**

x x x
Crusaders
RAYMOND OF TOULOUSE

BETHLEHEM

15. **The Fatimid garrison construct nine mangonels to bombard Raymond of Toulouse's siege tower.**

N

An enthroned prince with his attendants and a horseman, on a Saljuq Turkish painted ceramic from Iran, dating from the 12th or early 13th century. (Reza Abbasi Museum, Tehran; author's photograph)

supplies. In other words they could not have returned if they had not found a friendly port. However, a Fatimid squadron promptly appeared outside Jaffa. One Christian ship escaped back to Latakia using both sails and oars but the others were beached within the harbour.

Apparently the naval commanders in Latakia had sent this small squadron loaded with military materials in the hope of reaching a suitable landing place behind Fatimid naval lines. It was an act of daring and was hailed as such outside Jerusalem. When the Fatimid fleet threatened to enter Jaffa, the Genoese sailors dismantled their vessels, took the most useful pieces of timber to Jerusalem and burned the rest.

One of these Genoese captains, Guglielmo Embriaco, was an engineer and he supervised the construction of a movable siege tower for Raymond of Toulouse using wood from the Genoese ships and their cargo. He similarly constructed a stone-throwing machine for Godfrey of Bouillon. The Genoese were, of course, well known for their skill in timber and rope technology, though Muslim captives did much of the heavy work.

Now Godfrey and the other Crusader commanders facing the northern wall of Jerusalem wanted a siege tower like that being constructed for Raymond, but they lacked suitable wood. Timber-cutters were sent north to the area around Nablus but it is unclear how much they found, though a foraging raid in this direction did capture food. Then the Crusaders had a stroke of luck. Tancred, who was suffering from dysentery, went into a cave to relieve himself in private, and there found a store of timber previously hidden by the Fatimid authorities. Consequently a second siege tower was constructed under the protection of Godfrey of Bouillon.

On 8 July the entire Crusader army, including non-combatants, walked round Jerusalem in a procession that culminated in sermons and a religious service on the Mount of Olives. This was not only to seek God's help but also to raise Crusader morale while depressing that of the Muslim and Jewish defenders. Crusader morale was raised – but that of the Fatimid garrison was not diminished.

During the night of 9/10 July Godfrey of Bouillon's siege tower was moved in sections to a position facing the eastern part of the northern wall. This had not previously been attacked and there is little evidence that it was weaker than other parts of the defences. It was, however, as far

as possible from the southwestern corner where Count Raymond of Toulouse would attack. Godfrey, Tancred and the two Roberts shifted left while Raymond moved a similar distance to his right. Iftikhar al-Dawla now had to divide his forces and he probably moved his headquarters to the Citadel approximately midway between those units protecting the northeastern and those protecting the southwestern walls.

The sources also indicate that he divided his stone-throwing mangonels, which would have taken some time. But the Fatimid garrison must have been aware of the southern threat where Raymond's siege-tower was being constructed. So, when the final attack came, it was opposed by nine mangonels bombarding Raymond's tower and five bombarding the northern siege-tower. The fact that only five faced Godfrey's tower might indicate that moving this tower from its construction site opposite the western end of the northern wall to the eastern end caught the defenders by surprise.

The final assault

The final Crusader assault lasted from 13 to 15 July 1099. The attackers now had stone-throwing engines of their own, reportedly hurling available blocks of marble from ruined buildings, though this should be treated with caution as the missiles thrown by a mangonel had to be of a very specific weight to be accurate. Crusader archers also shot flaming arrows at straw bales with which the defenders tried to protect their wall from mangonel attack. As Raymond d'Aguilers stated: 'A young man shot arrows ablaze with cotton pads against the ramparts of the Saracens which defended against the wooden tower of Godfrey and the two Counts [on the north side]. Soon mounting flames drove the defenders from the ramparts.' This enabled the Crusaders to get onto the northern wall on 15 July and according to the *Gesta Francorum* a knight named Lethold was the first to do so. Once inside the city the attackers went berserk, slaughtering any Muslim or Jew they found. Raymond's Provençals were having a harder time attacking the southern wall. As

THE MASSACRE IN JERUSALEM (pages 78–79)

When the Crusaders broke into Jerusalem many went berserk, slaughtering the Muslim and Jewish inhabitants regardless of age, sex and whether or not they were civilians or soldiers. Some of the worst slaughter took place in and around the Aqsa Mosque (1) on the Haram al-Sharif or what Christians and Jews call the Temple Mount. Defenders who fled to this area were simply massacred along with great numbers of civilians. Most of the killing seems to have been done by northern European Crusaders since it was they who first broke into Jerusalem and first reached the Haram al-Sharif. They included Normans and northern French (2), and men from what are now the Benelux countries, eastern France and western Germany (3). Those who were slaughtered included the urban population of Jerusalem (4), fleeing soldiers (5), and local peasants who had sought safely within Jerusalem (6). Arab and Islamic sources were, however, particularly appalled by the Crusaders' indiscriminate killing of woman and children (7), which was totally contrary to Islamic rules of warfare. Muslim religious leaders (8) were also targeted with particular savagery, as the Arab chronicler Ibn al-Athir confirmed; 'In the Masjid al-Aqsa [at the southern end of the Haram al-Sharif] the Franks slaughtered more than 70,000 people, amongst them a large number of *imams* and

Muslim scholars, devout and ascetic men who had left their homelands to live lives of pious seclusion in the Holy Places. The Franks stripped the Dome of the Rock of more than 40 silver candelabras (9), each of them weighing 3,600 *drams*, and a great silver lamp weighing 44 Syrian *rutl*, as well as 150 smaller silver candelabra and more than 20 gold ones, as well as a great deal other booty.' Other Islamic religious scholars who somehow escaped the conquerors' initial frenzy were murdered later. One man named al-Rumayli was offered for a ransom of 1,000 *dinars*, but when this could not be raised the Crusaders stoned him to death several weeks later. What seems so extraordinary from a modern point of view is less the massacre itself, which was carried out in a religious frenzy by men who had themselves suffered enormously on their way to Jerusalem, but the way it was glorified by chroniclers writing after the hysteria had subsided. The anonymous author of the *Gesta Francorum* described how the slaughter of Muslims in the 'Temple' area continued on the day after the city fell, killing those who had escaped the carnage inside the Aqsa Mosque; 'In the morning our men climbed up cautiously on to the roof of the Temple and attacked the Saracens, both male and female, and beheaded them with unsheathed swords. The other Saracens threw themselves from the Temple.' (Christa Hook)

An episode in the 'Story of King Arthur' showing the siege of a castle, on a relief carving dating from the start of the 12th century. (*In situ* north door of the Cathedral, Modena)

Raymond d'Aguilers again recorded: *At midday we were in a state of confusion, a phase of fatigue and hopelessness brought on by the stubborn resistance of many remaining defenders, the lofty and seemingly impregnable walls, and the overwhelming defensive skills of the defenders ... At the very moment when a council debated the wisdom of withdrawing our machines, since many were burned or badly shattered, a knight whose name is unknown to me signalled with his shield from the Mount of Olives to the Count and others to move forward.*

So Raymond's men attacked again and this time the defence collapsed. Ibn al-Athir does, however, indicate that the southern siege tower was burned but that immediately afterwards the northern wall was breached. Its defenders asked for help from the southern sector, whereupon the entire defence fell apart. Some troops defending the southern wall withdrew to the Citadel to rejoin their commander, Iftikhar al-Dawla. There, as Ibn al-Athir recorded: *A band of Muslims barricaded themselves in the Mihrab Da'ud* [the Citadel] *and fought on for several days. They were granted their lives in return for surrendering. The Franks honoured their word and the group left by night for Ascalon.*

Raymond and his followers behaved better that those Crusaders who broke into the north of Jerusalem. Instead of massacring the Jews, Raymond took many captive. Others were permitted to leave under safe conduct with what remained of the Fatimid garrison. Around the Mount Zion area in southwestern Jerusalem other defenders were refused quarter. Here, according to Raymond d'Aguilers: *The Saracens fought fiercely with Raymond's forces as if they had not been defeated ... Some of the*

Beneath the central dome of the Aqsa Mosque in Jerusalem, showing mosaic decoration made under Fatimid rule around AD1035.

pagans were mercifully beheaded, others pierced by arrows plunged from towers, and yet others, tortured for a long time, were burned to death in searing flames. Piles of heads, hands and feet lay in the houses and streets, and indeed there was a running to and fro of men and knights over the corpses.

Worse still was the carnage on the Temple Mount. Defenders who fled to this area where simply massacred along with great numbers of civilians. The *Gesta Francorum* describes how the slaughter of Muslims in the 'Temple' area continued the following day: *In the morning our men climbed up cautiously on to the roof of the Temple and attacked the Saracens, both male and female, and beheaded them with unsheathed swords. The other Saracens threw themselves from the Temple.* Ibn al-Athir confirmed the carnage and looting: *In the Masjid al-Aqsa* [at the southern end of the Haram al-Sharif] *the Franks slaughtered more than 70,000 people, amongst them a large number of imams and Muslim scholars, devout and ascetic men who had left their homelands to live in pious seclusion in the Holy Places. The Franks stripped the Dome of the Rock of more than forty silver candelabra, each of them weighing 3,600 drams, and a great silver lamp weighing 44 Syrian rutl, as well as 150 smaller silver candelabra and more than 20 gold ones, as well as much other booty.*

The worst massacre of Jews took place in the main synagogue, where the community had gathered for sanctuary. The Crusaders burned the building with the people still inside. Other Jews were sent to Italy as slaves, though most were killed on the way. Some Christians had remained in Jerusalem during the siege and they sheltered in the Church of the Holy Sepulchre. Some sources indicate that surviving Jews and local Christians were forced to clean the bodies of slain Crusaders.

After such slaughter the disposal of the dead became a priority in the summer heat of Palestine. Some Crusader religious leaders ordered their men to clear away the enemy corpses as an act of penance. Surviving Muslims were also forced to drag the dead out of Jerusalem and make piles, reportedly 'as big as houses', in front of the city gates where the bodies were then burned.

The impact of these appalling events varied in different parts of the Islamic world. Ibn al-Athir described how refugees arrived in Baghdad during the Islamic holy month of Ramadan. There they told the 'Abbasid Caliph's ministers a story that 'wrung their hearts and brought tears to their eyes'. On Friday, the day of prayer, some leading refugees went to the Congregational Mosque and begged for help, 'weeping so that their hearers wept with them as they described the suffering of the Muslims in that Holy City, the men killed, the women and children taken prisoner, the homes pillaged. Because of the terrible hardships they had suffered, they were allowed to break the fast [of Ramadan].'

THE BATTLE OF ASCALON

Fatimid naval domination of the coast could not have saved the Holy City but it did enable the Grand Vizier al-Afdal to assemble a substantial army at Ascalon in an attempt to raise the Crusader siege. It arrived too late, however, because of the huge logistical difficulties of getting large numbers of troops across Sinai from Egypt to Palestine. Normally this took two months, so al-Afdal may have started to assemble the army in mid-June, the moment when the Crusaders' intentions became brutally clear with their first attack upon Jerusalem. The Crusaders, of course, intensified their

Fully armoured cavalry attacking fully armoured infantry on the late 11th-century Anglo-Norman *Bayeux Tapestry*. (Tapestry Museum, Bayeux)

siege when they leaned that a relief force was approaching Ascalon, namely in early July.

The army that assembled outside Ascalon was clearly formidable, though not as large as some Crusader chroniclers suggested. It probably consisted of the professional forces based in Cairo under al-Afdal's immediate Command. These, according to Ibn al-Qalanisi, made camp outside Ascalon on 4 August. They were joined by local forces from the *Sahil* or coastal lowlands of Palestine and 'awaited the arrival of the fleet and the bedouin'. The latter were the tribes of southern Palestine, which played a leading role in the defence of these regions and would continue to defend Ascalon until it fell to the Crusaders over half a century later. However, the Crusaders attacked al-Afdal before his reinforcements arrived. 'The fleet' probably meant transport ships bringing supplies and materials for siege machinery.

Although the evidence is scanty, the Fatimid army probably camped on the northeastern side of Ascalon where there are sources of drinkable water. Ascalon itself had a strong wall pierced by powerful gates. It stood above low cliffs and there was a rather exposed roadstead for shipping immediately north of the city itself. The terrain outside the walls varied from open sand and sandy scrub with scattered trees, to orchards and olive groves. There were also areas of grazing or pasture.

The text of the message that al-Afdal sent to the Crusaders in Jerusalem apparently complained more about the slaughter of local Muslim inhabitants than the Crusaders' seizure of the Holy City. Perhaps the Fatimid Grand Vizier thought that a negotiated agreement could still be reached and did not want to break off relations entirely. However, the invaders were now in a state of religious euphoria. Many of the rank-and-file may even have believed they were involved in events leading up to the End of the World. So the Crusader leaders gave al-Afdal's representatives a noncommittal reply then assembled their forces to march against the Fatimid army hard on the heels of the returning ambassadors. Non-combatants remained behind.

Raymond d'Aguilers recorded a bizarre story current amongst the Crusaders that al-Afdal planned to capture all the Franks under 20 years of age: *He would, so rumour held, mate the young Frankish males with women of his race and the Frankish women with males of his land and thereby breed a warrior race from Frankish stock.* This garbled misunderstanding reflected the traditional Islamic practice of recruiting elite troops from young slaves or captives. On 10 August Crusader troops assembled at Yibna (Yavne), close to the coast and almost halfway from Jaffa to Ascalon. The choice of Yibna suggests that they wanted to stay in contact with Jaffa as well as Jerusalem. Raymond d'Aguilers described the advance: *The leaders issued a call to the able bodied, prayed to God, marched out of Jerusalem in full armour carrying the Holy Lance and on the same day came to the plains. On the following day* [11 August] *our united armies moved forward in squadrons with guards drawn up on all sides.*

The huge Bab al-Futuh gate in the northern walls of what was the Fatimid palace-city of al-Qahira, or Cairo. It was built between 1087 and 1092 by Badr al-Jamali, predecessor and father of the Grand Vizier al-Afdal. (Author's photograph)

In fact the Crusader contingents now formed up in what was, for western European troops, an unusual array. It consisted of nine divisions, each apparently in a three-by-three formation of horse and foot so that it could face an attack from any direction, a formation that later became a classic Crusader tactic. By time of the battle of Ascalon the invaders were veterans of warfare against the Turks if not against the Fatimids. However, this early form of 'fighting march' has little in common with Byzantine tactics in hostile territory. Rather it seems much closer to a formation used by Turkish and Chinese armies in Central Asia, and perhaps also in Saljuq Iran. Perhaps the three-by-three box was learned from captured Turks who had been 'turned', some of whom were clearly now with the Crusader host.

The Crusaders made contact with Fatimid outposts late on 11 August and captured many of the enemy's flocks near, or more likely south of, Isdud (Ashdod). Raymond d'Aguilers adds details: *At sunset we approached a river which is on the road from Jerusalem to Ascalon, and we saw Arabs pasturing flocks of sheep and large herds of cattle and camels. So we sent two hundred knights to reconnoitre, because the large number of Arabs and livestock made us believe that a fight would ensue ... The Arab herdsmen fled at the sight of our knights ... Following their flight we seized unbelievable amounts of booty, and killed and captured a few Arabs. Since it was late in the day we pitched camp and then we compelled the captives to reveal their plans, state of preparation, and their numbers ... They* [the captives] *added that the amir* [al-Afdal] *who was camped five leagues away, would march against us the next day ... Orders were given throughout the army that all should be prepared for battle at dawn, that each man join the forces of his leader, and that no one should touch booty until after the battle.*

Raymond d'Aguilers' river may have been the Sukhray (Lakhis) or Ibtah (Evtah), which are the only streams between Isdud and Ascalon. This would have put the Crusaders' camp 10–15 kilometres north of Ascalon.

By now a substantial Fatimid fleet was probably moored north of Ascalon. On the other hand the Fatimid army was undoubtedly caught unprepared outside the fortified walls of Ascalon. As the Crusaders approached, the Fatimids attempted to form their battle array. The professionals of al-Afdal's Cairo regiments should have had little difficulty doing so but the army also included the Ascalon militia and local volunteers. One can imagine the confusion caused by large numbers of part-time soldiers hurrying out of Ascalon and attempting to take their positions north of the city. The Fatimid army was organised and trained along traditional lines developed during the Golden Age of the 'Abbasid Caliphate in the 9th and 10th centuries. These emphasised caution, careful preparation, largely static battle tactics and a considerable reliance upon a military bureaucracy; fine virtues under some circumstances but not when a fanatical foe was rapidly advancing from a few kilometres away.

The *Gesta Francorum*'s reference to Fatimid troops, 'each of them hanging around his neck a bottle from which he could drink', suggests that even under these desperate circumstances many thought they had time to prepare for a long hot day. On the Crusader side preparations for battle were quicker, as Raymond d'Aguilers wrote: *At the crack of dawn the alert was called to battle-ranks by the blare of trumpets and horns. Thus we set out at day break with guards arranged on all sides as previously reported ... The Arabs remained in their camp in the belief that at news of their coming we would remain close to our*

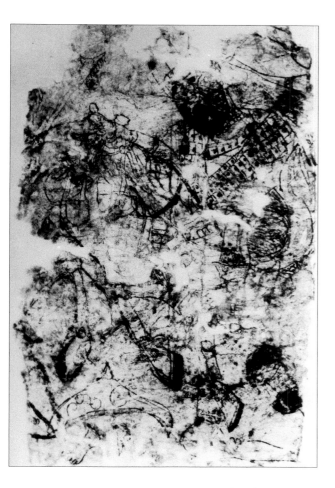

Fragment of painted paper from the abandoned Cairo suburb of Fustat, showing two horsemen shaking hands above the carnage of battle, probably made in the 11th or early 12th century. (Keir Collection, London)

walls [Jerusalem]. Reports had come to them of the slaughter and flight of the herders and it brought this response, 'The Franks came for booty and will now return.' They had daily reports on desertions from Jerusalem, the small size of our army, and the enfeebled state of our people and horses … We moved forwards in nine ranks … and God multiplied his army to the point that we seemed equal to the Arab forces. This miracle came when the animals we had freed formed herds, and without a directing hand followed us, stood when we stood, ran when we ran, and marched forward when we marched forward.

The presence of these animal herds may not have been a case of dumb beasts preferring the company of Christians. It might be an unrecorded example of ex-Saljuq soldiers contributing to the Crusader tactics, since the driving of animals into enemy lines was common in earlier Islamic warfare. The only surviving letter from this period of the First Crusade was sent in September 1099 as an official account of the expedition and also described how herds of camels, cattle and sheep charged the enemy.

The host formed its battle array with Raymond of Toulouse on the right, Tancred, Robert of Normandy and Robert of Flanders in the centre, and Godfrey of Bouillon on the left, then attacked before the Fatimids had properly assembled. What happened next is hidden in the dust of those remarkable animal herds. Fulcher of Chartres indicated that Crusader infantry archers shot at advancing Fatimids before their own knights countercharged. This would suggest that Fatimid cavalry tried to slow the enemy attack because their own infantry was not ready to receive a charge. Any such pre-emptive stroke clearly failed and the Fatimid line, insofar as it yet existed, was broken. As Raymond d'Aguilers continued: *The Arabs, seeing the slaughter of many of their comrades and the eager and secure ransacking of their camp, gave up the fight and decided, 'Since we must flee, why delay?' … Consequently, with morale broken the Arabs with a few exceptions returned to Ascalon.*

The Fatimid left flank seemingly fell back to the coast, seeking refuge aboard ships moored in the roadstead but pursued by Raymond of Toulouse's division. When the Fatimid centre collapsed Tancred and Robert of Normandy took al-Afdal's camp. The Fatimid right wing probably fled south pursued by Godfrey of Bouillon. Fatimid troops who reportedly sought refuge in sycamore trees were probably from this right wing. They were smoked out or shot by arrows. However, it is possible these soldiers were attempting to hinder Crusader pursuit by establishing ambushes in thickets or close-cover, as described in a surviving Fatimid tactical manual. Muslim casualties were clearly high. According to Ibn al-Qalanisi: *About 10,000 foot soldiers, volunteers and people of the town were massacred, and the camp was plundered … It is said that the death toll amongst the*

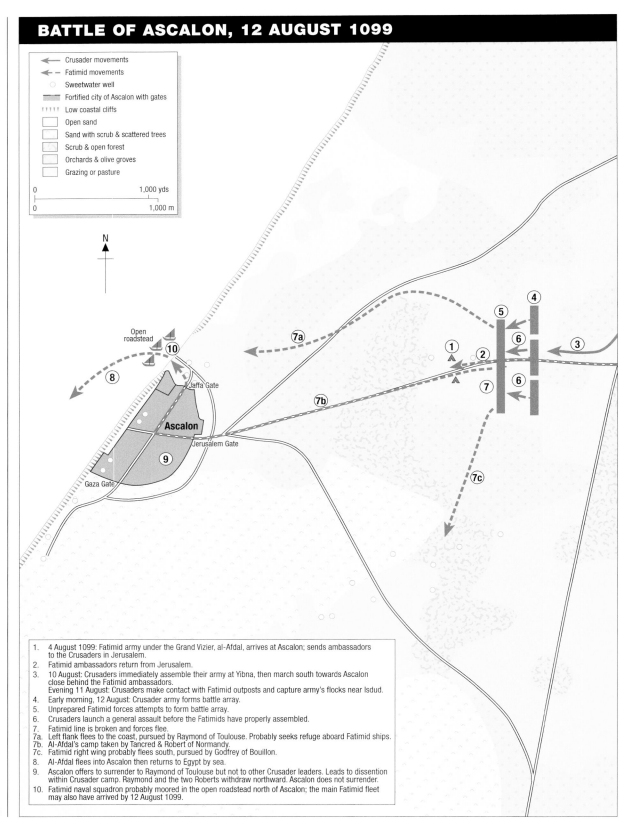

Key

- Crusader movements
- Fatimid movements
- Sweetwater well
- Fortified city of Ascalon with gates
- Low coastal cliffs
- Open sand
- Sand with scrub & scattered trees
- Scrub & open forest
- Orchards & olive groves
- Grazing or pasture

0 — 1,000 yds
0 — 1,000 m

N

Open roadstead

Jaffa Gate

Ascalon

Jerusalem Gate

Gaza Gate

1. 4 August 1099: Fatimid army under the Grand Vizier, al-Afdal, arrives at Ascalon; sends ambassadors to the Crusaders in Jerusalem.
2. Fatimid ambassadors return from Jerusalem.
3. 10 August: Crusaders immediately assemble their army at Yibna, then march south towards Ascalon close behind the Fatimid ambassadors.
   Evening 11 August: Crusaders make contact with Fatimid outposts and capture army's flocks near Isdud.
4. Early morning, 12 August: Crusader army forms battle array.
5. Unprepared Fatimid forces attempts to form battle array.
6. Crusaders launch a general assault before the Fatimids have properly assembled.
7. Fatimid line is broken and forces flee.
7a. Left flank flees to the coast, pursued by Raymond of Toulouse. Probably seeks refuge aboard Fatimid ships.
7b. Al-Afdal's camp taken by Tancred & Robert of Normandy.
7c. Fatimid right wing probably flees south, pursued by Godfrey of Bouillon.
8. Al-Afdal flees into Ascalon then returns to Egypt by sea.
9. Ascalon offers to surrender to Raymond of Toulouse but not to other Crusader leaders. Leads to dissention within Crusader camp. Raymond and the two Roberts withdraw northward. Ascalon does not surrender.
10. Fatimid naval squadron probably moored in the open roadstead north of Ascalon; the main Fatimid fleet may also have arrived by 12 August 1099.

A collection of late 11th-century Palestinian Arab jewellery that was buried in a vault in Ascalon as the Crusader hordes approached in AD1099.

people of Ascalon, including witnesses [men of sufficient status to carry weight in a law court], *residents* [prosperous citizens], *tradesmen and* ahdath [ordinary militiamen] *reached 2,700, quite apart from the* ajnad [garrison] *of the city.*

The Fatimid Grand Vizier fled into Ascalon with his *hawass* or staff, but the sources disagree whether he immediately withdrew to Cairo, leaving the local leadership to negotiate a surrender, or himself conducted preliminary talks. At this point one of the previously captured Saljuq soldiers emerged from the shadows of history. Raymond d'Aguilers wrote his story: *Raymond decided to send Bohemond, a Turk, to the* amir [al-Afdal] *with a plan for peace but also to remind him that he had been reluctant to free Jerusalem and had fought against us. Bohemond was, at the same time, to observe the situation and to see whether the* amir *planned to flee or to fight, and how he reacted to his defeat. Bohemond, though a Turk, spoke several languages, was clever and shrewd as well as loyal to us. He was called Bohemond because the great Bohemond* [of Taranto] *received him at the baptismal font when he turned apostate and came to us with his wife and weapons.*

Other versions suggest that Iftikhar al-Dawla, as governor of Ascalon, prepared to surrender the city, but then recognised the deepening divisions amongst his Crusader opponents. Apparently the city offered to surrender to Raymond of Toulouse but not to other Crusader leaders who were seen as responsible for massacring the population of Jerusalem. Raymond had also negotiated Iftikhar al-Dawla's surrender in Jerusalem, where he kept his word by allowing the governor and his men to reach Ascalon safely. However, this insistence caused dissention in the Crusader camp. As a result Raymond and the two Roberts withdrew northwards and the surrender of Ascalon never actually took place.

THE AFTERMATH

The success of the First Crusade resulted from its superior numbers and cohesion while the failure of Islamic forces was due to the fragmented and uncoordinated response of their rulers. The only real exception to this scenario was the Crusaders' remarkable defeat of Kür-Bugha's allied army outside Antioch. Here, however, a large part of the Islamic army abandoned the field as a result of a decision to deny Kür-Bugha a victory that could have made him 'over-powerful'. The Crusaders almost invariably demonstrated greater motivation that appeared, to their foes, to be religious fanaticism. There is no real evidence that western European Crusaders enjoyed technological or tactical superiority. In fact the reverse seems more likely to have been the case. Even where warhorses were concerned the popular image of European knights on larger horses that knocked over their opponents' supposedly smaller horses is a myth. On the contrary the professional elite of the main Saljuq and Fatimid armies probably had bigger horses than those of most Crusader knights. Furthermore the Crusaders had lost virtually all their original mounts by the time they reached Jerusalem.

Almost immediately after the First Crusade's defeat of the Fatimid army outside Ascalon, the majority of Crusaders started returning home. Most travelled overland to northern Syria before taking ship westward because the Fatimid fleet still dominated the coasts of Palestine and Lebanon. Eventually no more than 300 or so knights and an unknown number of infantry stayed to defend Jerusalem, Ramlah and Haifa; the nucleus of the future Kingdom of Jerusalem.

Thereafter four Crusader States gradually emerged from the County of Edessa and Principality of Antioch in the north, through the County of Tripoli to the Kingdom of Jerusalem in the south. Relations between the Principality of Antioch and the Byzantine Empire, which still claimed this area, remained complex and tense while the Kingdom of Lesser Armenia also emerged in Cilicia between Antioch and Byzantine territory.

Jerusalem was now badly damaged and was inhabited by only a few hundred Crusader settlers, mostly living around the Church of the Holy Sepulchre. Nor could the tiny garrison man all its gates and towers. Most of the indigenous Arab Christian population had not returned following the siege, being regarded as suspect by the Crusaders, while the Muslims and Jews had been slaughtered. Meanwhile the Blessed Gerard was still in charge of the hospices from which the Crusader Order of the Hospitallers later developed. It was not until after further campaigns by

Two of the lost 12th-century stained-glass windows in St Denis, Paris, illustrated the defeat of the Fatimid army outside Ascalon. A: Battle outside Ascalon. B: Fatimids flee into Ascalon.

King Baldwin I in 1115–16 that the long-established Christian communities on the eastern bank of the river Jordan were encouraged to settle in Jerusalem. This resulted in a mass exodus that ruined ancient Christian towns such as Madaba and Umm al-Rasas. Most of these incomers took over abandoned properties in what had been the old Jewish quarter in the northeastern corner of the city.

The acquisition of horses remained a vital concern since the Crusader settlers were desperately short of remounts and still seemed unable to acquire any by sea. Other reinforcements did, however, come by ship in the period immediately after the conquest of Jerusalem. These included a Norwegian fleet led by the brother of King Magnus, which arrived in time to help the Crusaders blockade Fatimid-held Sidon. A Venetian fleet had set sail from Italy in the autumn of 1099 and reached Jaffa in late June 1100.

Despite a revived threat from the Normans of southern Italy, Byzantine forces stabilised the situation in western Anatolia by 1105 having reconquered significant territory from the Turks. Other Byzantine forces regained the Black Sea coast but the Emperor Alexios I died before his great design was accomplished. In fact the Anatolian interior was never regained and, despite the Byzantines' best efforts, the Turks would, ultimately, triumph.

Armenian hopes for the future were similarly ill founded, though the Kingdom of Lesser Armenia would survive for several centuries. To the east the Danishmandids annexed Malatya while Kahramanmaras and Kaysun-Ra'ban were taken by the Crusaders. Armenians did continue to play a significant role in Syria and an even more important one in Fatimid Egypt. A Muslim Armenian named Yaruktash even briefly controlled Aleppo in the 1120s while another Muslim Armenian held power in the Hawran area of what is now southern Syria and northern Jordan between the Turkish ruler of Damascus and Crusader Kingdom of Jerusalem.

The biggest losers as a result of the First and subsequent Crusades were undoubtedly the indigenous Middle Eastern Christians, the greatest sufferers being the Syrian Christians. When the First Crusaders took Jerusalem in 1099 they found the Greek Orthodox higher clergy had withdrawn to Cyprus because of the Saljuq conquest and had not yet returned. So the Crusaders replaced them with Catholics. This was one

St George attacking the infidels while Crusaders pray on the other side. This Anglo-Norman carving probably illustrates the conquest of Antioch or the defeat of Kür-Bugha's army. (*In situ* parish church, Fordington; author's photograph)

of several reasons why the Arabic-speaking, Greek Orthodox Christian community in Palestine remained mistrustful of the Latin, Catholic, western European Crusaders. In contrast the Maronite Christians of Lebanon reached a compromise with the Catholic Crusaders and became their allies.

Apart from the massacre of the Jewish inhabitants of Jerusalem, the Jews of the Middle East did not suffer the same serious long-term consequences as the Christians. Not surprisingly, their loyalty to the Fatimid Caliphate was strengthened. In the short term, however, there was considerable suffering, as shown in a surviving letter found in the Cairo *Genizah* some years ago: *News has reached us that amongst those who were ransomed from the Franks and remained in Ascalon, some are in danger of dying of want. Others remained in captivity, and yet others were killed before the eyes of the rest who were themselves killed afterwards with all manner of torture in order to give vent to his* [the enemy's] *anger on them.*

'The Emperor Alexios I presenting the *Panoplia dogmatike* to Christ', in a 12th-century Byzantine manuscript. (*Panoplia dogmatike*, Cod. 666, f. 2v, Vatican Library, Rome)

Later the same letter added: *Now amongst those who have reached safety* [in Cairo] *are some who escaped on the second and third days following the battle and left with the governor who was granted safe conduct. And others who, after having been caught by the Franks, remained in their hands for some time and escaped in the end, these are but few. The majority consists of those who were ransomed. To our sorrow, some of them ended their lives under all kinds of suffering and affliction.*

There are also interesting references to Jews being captured by the Crusaders at Antioch the previous year. Many Jews fled to Ascalon and the Ascalon community survived until the city fell to the Crusaders in 1153. The Jews of Ascalon and Egypt also ransomed many books looted by the Crusaders when they took Jerusalem.

Reactions to the Crusader conquests varied in different parts of the Islamic world. In Anatolia

the threat from Crusader Antioch in the south and Byzantine reconquest in the east led to a short-lived reconciliation between Qïlïch Arslan and Danishmandids, resulting in the defeat of a Crusade in 1100–02. Despite widespread apathy in the eastern parts of the Great Saljuq Sultanate, some Islamic scholars tried to rally support for an effort to drive out the invaders. Poets also bemoaned the lack of response to these awful events. An Iraqi named Abu'l-Muzaffar al-Abiwardi urged his compatriots to help their Syrian and Palestinian brothers:

> Dare you slumber in the blessed shade of safety, where life is as soft as an
> orchard flower?
> How can you sleep at a time of disasters that would waken any sleeper?
> While your Syrian brothers can only sleep on the backs of their warhorses, or
> in the bellies of vultures!

Syrian attitudes to the First Crusade are similarly reflected in a poem by Ibn al-Khayyat after the fall of Jerusalem:

> How long will this go on?
> For the polytheists have overflowed like a flood, so great that even the sea
> fears it.
> Armies like mountains have stormed out of the land of the Ifranj, to bring
> about our destruction.
> How many young women have started to beat their throats and cheeks in
> fear,
> And mothers of young girls who have not yet known the heat of day, nor
> suffered cold at night?
> They are almost wasting away from fear, and dying from sadness and
> painful worry.

The success of the First Crusade has sometimes been blamed on the fragmentation of the Great Saljuq Sultanate. Yet the Sultanate was not collapsing in 1098–99. It might be more true to say that the First Crusade contributed to Great Saljuq decline. Kür-Bugha's defeat and loss of both prestige and military power may, in fact, have ended the last chance of restoring the Great Saljuq state.

It took a long time to motivate a counter-*jihad* to mirror the enthusiasm of the Crusade. Nevertheless, there was widespread outrage because this invasion was so different from previous 'civilised' wars between Byzantines and Muslims. Eventually there was a Sunni Muslim revival that resulted in a hardening of attitudes to non-Muslims. It was also characterised by less tolerance of Shi'a Muslims and any who were seen as unorthodox or heretical.

The impact of the Crusade was less immediate for the Fatimid Caliphate. In addition to the Jews of Jerusalem, much of the Arab Islamic elite of Palestine migrated to Ascalon after the First Crusade. The greatest fear amongst these Muslims was that their women would fall into the hands of the uncivilised westerners. In immediate military terms the impact of al-Afdal's defeat was a thorough reform of the Fatimid army. He also placed one of his own sons in command of Fatimid forces in Palestine. Perhaps this was when the previous governor, Iftikhar al-Dawla, left Fatimid service and maybe moved to the castle of Abu Qubays in northern Syria.

THE BATTLEFIELDS TODAY[3]

Seated Islamic prince holding a cup, on a fragment of woollen textile, probably from 10th-century Egypt. (Textile Museum, Washington; author's photograph)

The First Crusade was a journey as much as a campaign. Several writers have attempted to follow in its footsteps, most notably Tim Severin, although his book[4] suffers from two drawbacks. The author tried to do the journey with a horse in order to understand the problems involved but unfortunately chose the wrong sort of animal. Secondly he made his journey at a time of considerable tension in the Middle East and so was unable to trace the Crusaders' route through Lebanon and most of what is now Israel.

Because western European historians have focused upon the extraordinary achievements of the First Crusaders themselves, much less attention has been given to the areas where their Byzantine allies and Islamic opponents assembled or campaigned. This resulted in an unbalanced understanding of the episode as a whole.

As far as this book is concerned the story began in Istanbul, which is a major tourist centre with abundant accommodation and good transport. Their first objective, now called Iznik, lies within the tourist zone of western Turkey. Beyond this anyone wishing to follow the Crusaders' route will be venturing into less developed territory. The roads are good and transport is readily available in the form of Turkey's hair-raising long-distance bus service or in marginally less terrifying *dolmus* 'shared taxis'. Unfortunately the correct site of the so-called battle of Dorylaeum is not a tourist spot. It is, in fact, partially covered by a lorry park and other industrial buildings. The Crusaders' subsequent route from Eskisehir (Dorylaeum) to some distance outside Afyon (Amorium) currently consists of primitive and often unsurfaced country roads. From Afyon to Konya (Iconium) and Kayseri the route largely, though not entirely, consists of modern roads. Each of these typically Turkish towns has abundant, cheap and friendly local hotels and the small restaurants that make travel through Turkey a delight.

Further east and into the Taurus mountains the roads become more difficult and, as Tim Severin found, the route taken by the Crusaders was not necessarily the same as that followed by the few surfaced roads across these rugged hills. Paradoxically the routes used by the Saljuqs and Danishmandids around Malatya and in their march westward to face the Crusaders appear to have followed those of several major intercontinental trunk roads. Back in the Taurus mountains efforts to follow the Crusaders can lead a venturesome driver up an 'improved' local road into what appears to be a minor mountain pass only to find that the 'improved' road degenerates into an animal track near the top. Completing such a

---

3 At the time of writing, Iraq has been invaded by American and British forces, so it might be some time before the information concerning Iraq in this chapter is once again relevant.
4 T. Severin, *Crusader: By Horse to Jerusalem* (London 1989).

challenging stretch of the route can be 'rewarding', though only after rejoining a proper road some distance down the other side of the pass.

Driving in Syria, either with one's own car or one hired locally, is much easier than driving in some parts of southeastern Turkey. The same is, or was, the case in Iraq. Here the roads may appear relatively few but they tend to be modern and well maintained. Small, friendly and cheap local hotels are similarly abundant in Syria, though less so in northern Iraq. There are also plenty of local eating places, though these are neither as abundant nor as varied as in Turkey. Following the routes taken by various Crusader contingents and those of their Islamic opponents is easy in Syria because these operations took place in the most populated and urbanised regions of the west and north. The battles and sieges took place in these same areas.

The Crusaders marched down the coast of Lebanon along a road that is now open to visitors, the only major obstacle being the closed border between Lebanon and Israel. Today even the region immediately north of this frontier, which was ravaged by Israeli invasion and occupation, is opening to visitors. The current situation in what was Palestine, and now consists of Israel proper plus the occupied Palestinian territories of the West Bank and Gaza Strip, is very different. Communications would normally be good and hotels adequate if rather few and far between in some areas. However, the present situation makes following in the footsteps of the Crusaders and their foes difficult and sometimes impossible.

BIBLIOGRAPHY

Lists of original sources are included in most modern accounts of the First Crusade, one of the most comprehensive being in J. France, *Victory in the East* (Cambridge 1994). Consequently the following bibliography concentrates on secondary works.

Andressohn, J.C., *The Ancestry and Life of Godfrey of Bouillon* (Bloomington 1947).

Aube, P., *Godefroy de Bouillon* (Paris 1985).

Azhari, T.K. El-, *The Saljuqs of Syria during the Crusades 463–549 AH/1070–1154 AD* (Berlin 1997).

Bachrach, B.S., 'The siege of Antioch: a study in military demography', *War in History,* VI (1999) 127–146.

Brett, M., 'The Battles of Ramla (1099–1105),' U. Vermeulen & D. De Smet (eds.), *Egypt and Syria in the Fatimid, Ayyubid and Mamluk Eras* (Leuven 1995) 17–37.

Brundage, J.A., 'The Army of the First Crusade and the Crusader Vow … ', *Medieval Studies,* XXXIII (1971) 334–343.

Bull, M., *Knightly Piety and the Lay Response to the First Crusade* (Oxford 1998).

Crawford, R.W., 'Ridwan the Maligned', in J. Kritsek (ed.), *The World of Islam: Studies in Honour of P.K. Hitti* (London 1960) 135–144.

Edde, A-M., 'Ridwan, prince d'Alep de 1095–1113', *Revue des Etudes Islamiques,* LIV (1986) 103–128.

Flori, J., 'Chevalerie et guerre sainte: les motivations des chevaliers de la première croisade', in D. Buschinger (ed), *La Guerre au Moyen-Age, realité et fiction, Medievales , VII* (Amiens 2000) 55–68.

Flori, J., *La Première Croisade* (Brussels 1997).

Foss, M., *People of the First Crusade* (1997).

France, J., 'An Unknown Account of the Capture of Jerusalem', *English Historical Review,* LXXXVII (1972) 771–783.

France, J., 'Technology and the Success of the First Crusade', in Y. Lav (ed.), *War and Society in the Eastern Mediterranean, 7th–15th centuries* (Leiden 1996) 163–176.

France, J., 'The Fall of Antioch during the First Crusade', in M. Balard (ed.), *Dei Gesta per Francos* (Aldershot 2001) 13–20.

France, J., *Victory in the East: A Military History of the First Crusade* (Cambridge 1994).

Goiten, S.D., 'Contemporary Letters on the Capture of Jerusalem by the Crusaders', *The Journal of Jewish Studies,* III–IV (1952) 162–177.

Hamblin, W.J., 'The Fatimid navy during the Early Crusades', *American Neptune,* XLVI (1986), 77–83.

Hill, J.H., & L.L. Hill, *Raymond IV, Count of Toulouse* (Syracuse 1962).

Krey, A.C., The *First Crusade: Accounts of Eye-Witnesses and Participants* (Princeton 1921; reprint Gloucester Mass. 1958).

Mullett, M.E., & D. Smythe, *Alexios I Komnenos* (Belfast 1996).

Murray, A.V., 'The Army of Godfrey of Bouillon; Structure and Dynamics of a contingent in the First Crusade', *Revue Belge de Philologie et d'Histoire,* LXX (1992) 301–329.

Nicholson, R.L., *Tancred: A Study of his Career and Work* (Chicago 1940).

Phillips, J. (ed), *The First Crusade, Origins and Impact: Proceedings of the Deus Vult Conference, London, Nov. 1995* (Manchester 1997).

Riley-Smith, J., *The First Crusade and the Idea of Crusading* (London 1986).

Riley-Smith, J., 'The Motives of the Earliest Crusaders and the Settlement of Latin Palestine, 1095–1100', *English Historical Review,* CCCLXXXIX (1983) 721–736.

Salibi, K.S., *Syria under Islam: Empire on Trial 634–1097* (Delmar 1977).

Severin, T., *Crusader: By Horse to Jerusalem* (London 1989).

Shepard, J., 'The English and Byzantium: A Study of the Role in the Byzantine Army in the Late Eleventh Century', *Traditio,* XXIX (1973) 53–92.

Sivan, R., 'Syro-Palestinian Refugees at the time of the Crusades', in B.Z. Kedar (ed), *The Crusaders in their Kingdom* (Jerusalem 1987).

Tritton, A.S., & H.A.R. Gibb, 'The First and Second Crusades from an Anonymous Syriac Chronicle', *Journal of the Royal Asiatic Society* (1933) 69–101.

Vandevoorde, M.A., 'Le première croisade et l'instillation de Francs en Orient', in G. Brunel & E. Lalou (eds), *Sources d'histoire medievales (IXe–milieu du XIV siècle)* (Paris 1992).

Yewdale, R.B., *Bohemund I, Prince of Antioch* (Princeton 1917).

INDEX

Figures in **bold** refer to illustrations

Acre 65
Adhémar, Bishop 55, 60
al-Afdal Ibn Badr al-Jamali 11, 18–19
    at Ascalon (1099) 82–7
    after Crusade 91
    on Crusaders' appearance 20
    and Jerusalem 61–5, 72–3
    plans 30
Africa, Fatimid relations with 11, 25
'Akkar 69, 70
al-Bira 46
Aleppo, Tutah Mosque 36
Alexios Komnenos I, Byzantine Emperor 16, **19**, **90**
    and Bohemond of Taranto 14
    before Crusade 7, 10
    during Crusade 31, 32, 33, 47–8
    strategy 28–9
Amadiyah 54
Anatolia
    Crusader march across 35, 41–7
    local politics 90–1
    operations map **46**
    Turkish and Byzantine struggle over 7–8, 9, 10, 47–8, 89
animals, Fatimid use in battle **42–4**, 85
Antioch (Antakya) **37**, **40**
    battle outside (1098) **53**, 56–60, **62–4**, 89, **90**
    after Crusade 14
    in Crusader strategy 29
    St Peter's grotto **41**
    siege and aftermath (1097–98) **40**, 48, 49–60, 65–8
Aqsa Mosque, Jerusalem **78–80**, 82
archery and archers **44**, 47, **62–4**
Ariha 45
Armenia 9, 10, 23, 41–5, 89
Armenians, in Fatimid armies 26, 72
armour **11**, **15**, **42–4**
    see also headwear; shields
'Artah 49
'Arthur, Story of King' **81**
Arwad island **59**
Ascalon **89**, **90**
Ascalon, battle of (1099) 83–7, **86**, **88**
Augustopolis, battle outside (1097) 41

Baghras 49
Bahram al-Armani 65, 71
Baldwin I, king of Jerusalem (formerly Baldwin of Boulogne, then count of Edessa) **15**, **18**, 41, 45, 47, 89
battlescenes **42–4**, **62–4**, **78–80**
Bayeux Tapestry **33**, **52**, **83**
Beirut 71
Berk Yaruq 18, 56

Bethlehem 71, **72**
bird's eye views **38–9**, **50–1**, **74–5**
Bohemond of Taranto 14
    Anatolia, march across 35
    at Antioch (1097–98) 54, 55, 56, 58, 60, 64
    Antioch, takes command of 68, 70
    at Dorylaeum (1097) 36, 44
    Latakia, attack on (1099) 71
    at Nicaea (1097) 32
    and Pisan fleet 48
    tomb **17**
bridges **54**
Byzantine army
    Crusade operations 32, 35–6, 41, 53–4
    composition and organisation 22
    leaders 16–17
    plans 28–9
    soldiers, Byzantine-type **11**, **61**, **90**
Byzantine Empire
    11th-century extent 7
    Anatolia, struggles over 7–8, 9, 10, 47–8, 89
    Armenia, annexation of 9
    Crusaders, split with 48, 53–4, 57
    Fatimids, relations with 29, 30, 31, 35
Byzantine fleet 33, 47, 48, 52, 69

Caesarea Mazacha (Kayseri) **27**, 41
Cairo (al-Qahira) 26, **84**
Çaka 7
calendar, Islamic 8
camels **42–4**
cavalry **85**
    at Antioch (1097–98) 57
    Islamic **41**
    Norman **52**, **68**, **83**
    relative strengths **88**
    Turkish ghulams 23–4, **42–4**, 60
chess pieces **55**
Christianity
    as Crusader inspiration 58, 60, **62–4**, 69, 70, 80, 83, **90**
    Easter celebrations **72**
    'Holy Lance' 58
    in Middle East 11, 89–90
    see also Jesus Christ; religion
Cilicia 41, 45–7
coins **18**
Coptic Church 11
Coxon (Göksun) 41
Crusader army
    Byzantines, relations with 31, 48, 53–4, 57
    composition and organisation 20–2
    division while on march 41
    Fatimids, relations with 35, 70
    leaders 14–16
    morality 80
    plans 27–8
    soldiers **22**, **40**, **62–4**, **73**, **78–80**

soldiers, Crusader-type **15**, **35**, **37**, **55**, **59**, **60**, **70**
Crusader fleets 48, 52, 55, 71, 73–6, 89

Danish Crusaders 48
Danishmandids 10
    after Crusade 14
    Crusade operations 32–3, 35–40, **42–4**
    Malatya, annexation of 89
    Saljuqs, relations with 48, 91
    strategy 30
David **71**
Daylami infantry 26
Dorylaeum, battle of (1097) **24**, 35–40, **42–4**, 92
Duqaq of Damascus 18, 48, 54, 57, 68

Edessa (Urfa) 23, **32**, 47, 57
Embriaco, Guglielmo 73, 76
English fleet 55

Fatimid army
    composition and organisation 11, 25–6, 84
    Crusade operations 72–82, 83–7, **88**
    leaders 18–19
    naffatun 26
    plans 30
    soldiers **18**, **45**, **48**, **85**, **88**
Fatimids
    Byzantines, relations with 29, 30, 31, 35
    before Crusade 11, 22
    Crusade's effect 91
    Crusaders, relations with 35, 70
    Jerusalem, capture of (1098) and rule 61–5, 72
    naval power 71, 76
Firuz al-Zarrad 55, 56
Flemish Crusaders 36
'Four Nourias' **69**
French Crusaders, northern 20
    Anatolia, march across 35
    at Antioch (1097–98) 58–9, **62–4**
    at Dorylaeum (1097) 35–6
    at Jerusalem (1099) **78–80**
    at Nicaea (1097) 33
    see also Provençal Crusaders
Fulcher of Chartres 33, 36, 44, 85

Genoese fleet 52, 73–6
George, St **61**, **90**
Gerard, 'The Blessed' 72, 88
German Crusaders 20, **62–4**, **78–80**
Gesta Francorum
    on al-Afdal 20
    on Antioch (1097–98) 57, 60
    on Ascalon (1099) 84
    on Dorylaeum (1097) 36, 40, 44
    on Jerusalem (1099) 80, 82
    on Pinarbasi (1097) 41

ghulams 23–4, **42–4**, 60
Godfrey of Bouillon 15
  at Antioch (1097–98) 56, 58–9
  at Ascalon (1099) 85
  and A'zaz 68
  at Dorylaeum (1097) 36
  and Jerusalem, march south to 70
  at Jerusalem (1099) 73, 76–7
  at Nicaea (1097) 32
Goliath **71**
Guynemer of Boulogne 45–7, 52

Harenc (Harim) 52, 54
headwear **15**, **48**
horse-harnesses **42–4**
horses, Crusader 45, 53, 54, **62–4**, 89
huntsmen **67**

Ibn al-Athir 49, 58, 59, 61, 68, 81, 82
Ibn al-Qalanisi 61, 83, 85–7
Iconium (Konya) 40–1, 47–8
Iftikhar al-Dawla 19
  after Ascalon (1099) 87
  after Crusade 91
  at Jerusalem (1099) 65, 72, 73, 77, 81
Isfahan **8**
Islam
  Crusade's effect 91
  Islamic princes **92**
  Isma'ili sect 8, 16
  massacre of religious leaders **78–80**
  Saljuq form 9
  sectarian rivalry 8, 9
  warfare, rules of 80
Istanbul **17**
Italian Crusaders 22, 35–6, 55, 56
Italian fleets 48, 52, 71, 73–6, 89

Jabala 70, 71
Jaffa 71, 73–6
al-Jamali, Badr 8, 11, 25, 84
Janah al-Dawla Husayn 18, 48–9, 59
Jerusalem **73**, **77**
  Aqsa Mosque **78–80**, **82**
  after Crusade 15
  Crusader march on 69–72
  Fatimid capture (1098) 61–5
  garrison 25
  history, layout and population 72
  siege (1099) and aftermath 72–82, **73**, **78–80**, 88–9
Jesus Christ **57**, **59**, **70**, **90**
jewellery **87**
Jews 11, 25, 60, 72, 80, 82, 90
John Axouchos 35
John Doukas 7–8, 47

Kahramanmaras (Marash) **31**, 41, 45
Kamal al-Din 52
Kayseri (Caesarea Mazacha) **27**, 41
Khalid ibn Wakas castle **49**
Kür-Bugha 18, 72
  Antioch, battle outside (1098) 53, 56–60, **62–4**, 88, **90**

Latakia 52, 70, 71, 76
Lebanon 70–1, **71**
Lotharingian Crusaders *see* German Crusaders

Ma'arat al-Nu'man 48, **58**, 68–9
Malatya (Melitene) **20**, 48, 92
Malik Shah, Great Saljuq Sultan 10, 11
Manzikert, battle of (1071) 7, 10
al-Maqrisi 61–5
Mar Matti (St Matthew), Monastery of **7**
Marash (Kahramanmaras) **31**, 41, 45
Melitene (Malatya) **20**, 48, 92
mihrabs **14**
Mosul **56**, **93**
mules **42–4**

naval operations 22, 45–7, 49–52, 98
  Byzantine 47, 48
  Jerusalem siege, naval support for 71, 73–6
  see also Byzantine fleet; Crusader fleets
Nicaea (Iznik) 10, **21**, **22**, **23**, 92
  siege (1097) 32–5
nomad encampments **10**
Norman Crusaders 20, **62–4**
Norman soldiers **52**, **68**, **83**
Norwegian fleet 89

Palestinian campaigns **66–7**, 71
Paulicians 40
Peasants' Crusade 29–30
Philomelium (Akshehir) 47–8
Philaretus 23, 47
pilgrims **13**
Pinarbasi 41
Pisan fleet 48, 71
prisoners, treatment of 33–5
Provençal Crusaders 14–15, 20
  operations 32, 36–7, 45, 58, **62–4**, 73, 77–81

Qilich Arslan I 10, 17
  after Crusades 40–1, 91
  at Dorylaeum (1097) 35–40, **42–4**
  and Iconium 47
  and Nicaea (1097) 32–3
  and Peasants' Crusade 29–30
  strategy 30

Raqqa, palace at **53**
Raymond d'Aguilers 40, 77–81, 81–2, 83, 84–5, 87
Raymond of Saint-Gilles, Count of Toulouse 14–15
  at Antioch (1097–98) 53, 58, 60, 64, 68
  at Ascalon (1099) and aftermath 85, 87
  at Malatya (Melitene) 20
  at Dorylaeum (1097) 36–7
  at Jerusalem (1099) 73, 76, 77–81
  Jerusalem, march south to 69
  at Nicaea (1097) 32
religion
  Fatimid armies 26
  in Jerusalem 72
  Middle East sects 11
  Turkish armies 24
  see also Christianity; Islam
religious pictures **24**, **57**, **59**, **70**, **90**
Ridwan Ibn Tutush of Aleppo 17, 18, 48–9, 54, 56–7, 72
roads, Turkey **25**
Robert, Count of Flanders 15
  at Antioch (1097–98) 54
  at Ascalon (1099) and aftermath 85, 87
  at Dorylaeum (1097) 36
  at Jerusalem (1099) 73, 77

Jerusalem, march south to 70
Robert, Count of Normandy ('Robert Curthose') 15, 32, 35, 73, 77, 85

St Denis, Paris, Church of **22**, **24**, **40**, **73**
Saint-Symeon (Samandag) 52
Salamiya, Old Mosque **16**
Saljuq armies
  composition and organisation 23–4
  Crusade operations **42–4**, 56–60
  ghulams 23–4, **42–4**, 60
  leaders 17–18
  plans 29–30
  soldiers **22**, **42–4**, **45**
  tactics 44
Saljuqs
  Anatolia, struggle for 7–8, 9, 10, 47–8, 89
  before Crusade 9, 10, 11
  civil wars 48–9, 72
  Crusade's effect 91
  Crusaders and Fatimids consider allegiance against 70
  Danishmandids, relations with 48, 91
  Jerusalem, loss to Fatimids (1098) 65
  rulers **28**, **76**
Shayzar 19, **65**
  siege 49
shields **41**, **60**
ships **9**, **23**, **33**, 46–7
Sidon (Saida) 65, 71, 89
siege weapons 61, 73, 76
Smyrna (Izmir) 47
Sökmen Ibn Artuk of Diyarbakr 48–9, 59, 61, 72
Stephen, Count of Blois 15, 32, 35, 36, 48, 53
Syria 11, 48–9, 66–7, 72

tactics 44, 84
Tafurs 21, 53, 68
Tancred 16
  at Antioch (1097–98) 52, 53, 54, 55
  at Ascalon (1099) 85
  and Bethlehem, seizure of (1099) 71
  Cilicia and east, march to 41, 47
  after Crusade 14
  at Jerusalem (1099) 73, 76, 77
Tatikios 16–17, 32, 35–6, 48, 53–4
Taurus mountains **29**, 41–5
Theodore, St **32**
T'oros (Theodore) Kurbalat 47
Tripoli 70–1
Turcomans 7, 10, 24
Turks *see* Danishmandids; Saljuqs
Tyre (Sur) 65

Urban II, Pope 20, 27, 55

Venetian fleet 89

waterwheels **69**
weapons
  crossbows **54**
  lances **52**
  maces **62–4**
  spears **60**
  swords **41**, **42–4**
  war-axes **37**
  see also archery and archers; siege weapons

Yaghi Siyan 17, 48–9, 55, 56

96